# REALITY CHRISTIANITY

## *A Study of II Corinthians*

### *Radiating Christ in Our Cracked Lives*

Nancy W. Carroll

Donelson Press, Nashville, Tennessee.

ISBN: 978-1-944066-85-7

Library of Congress Control Number: 2021944327

Printed in the United States

# Table of Contents

## TO THOSE WHO LONG FOR THE "REAL" THING:

In our increasingly "virtual reality world," we often wonder what or who is real. It is a battle in our Christian culture to be real with one another, God, and ourselves.

Have you experienced someone with a real relationship with God? As you see that person, you see more of the reality of God. You long for what he or she has. But you also wonder if you'd be willing to go through what that person has experienced or suffered to radiate Jesus Christ in such a real way.

Paul shows what it means to be real in II Corinthians, even when that means facing suffering, failure, criticism, and weakness. He reveals the truth that we can, with unveiled faces, radiate the glory of God to those around us as we embrace Jesus Christ and his power in our broken, weak, real lives. II Corinthians deals with the paradox of God's grace being sufficient (even activated) in our weakness. As Rev. Bob Flayhart says, "Grace does not fix us but is the means by which broken people, with broken lives, live in a broken world with hope."

## My Prayer for You

I pray that in recognizing our realities and embracing Christ, we can live in this broken world with hope. In this 13-week study, I pray you will find the real Christ and drop your masks to reveal the real you which will radiate His life to those around you.

How do we get there? God will use His Holy Word, His Holy Spirit, and His holy people to transform you week by week. I pray that you will be compelled by the love of Christ to fully open yourself to the three layers of this study: your personal study time in the book of II Corinthians, teaching time, and the small group time of sharing, fellowship, and prayer.

## Personal Study Time

Each weekly lesson is divided into five days that will take you about 10 to 15 minutes to complete. For those of you whose "reality" is that you hunger to be in God's Word but are continually frustrated by the lack of time, we have created a "Bible Study Express" approach which allows you to get through the lesson more quickly. Just answer the questions with an asterick (*).

The lesson uses Head/Heart/Hand questions for studying, believing, and applying Scripture. I pray God's Word works through your **head** (your intellect, what you think and believe), your **heart** (your inner being, what you feel and who you are), and your **hands** (what flows out of your life in response to what you think, believe and feel) so that God's reality would radiate through you, as it says in II Corinthians 3:16-18: *But when one turns to the Lord, the veil is removed. Now the Lord is the Spirit, and where the Spirit of the Lord is, there is freedom. And we all, with unveiled face, beholding the glory of the Lord, are being transformed into the same image from one degree of glory to another. For this comes from the Lord who is the Spirit.*

## Personal Discovery Sheet

At the end of each weekly lesson, you are invited to complete an *optional* Personal Discovery Sheet to explore the Scriptures for the week on your own. You'll find a step-by-step explanation of these sheets on page 16.

## Teaching Time

For those who want to lead or teach, a separate Teacher/Facilitator guide is available with additional notes and suggestions for leading a small group and teaching II Corinthians. The goal of the study and teaching time to help you see who the real God is and help to see your own "reality." Pray that only His truth will be spoken, simply, graciously, and in the power of the Holy Spirit in a way that will give you hope and transformation.

## Small Group Time

Although you can do this study on your own, it helps to study this with others. We want you to have a safe place where you can struggle and pray, love and learn together, and laugh and gain perspective on the realities you are in. Ideally, each week you'll break into small groups with leaders who will facilitate the weekly questions and will pray for and with you.

## Prayer Journal

At the end of this study, you'll find pages to record prayer requests for yourself and those in your small group.

As you begin this "Reality Christianity" study, pray for God to reveal Himself to you in a real and glorious way during this time. Pray that you will be daily renewed and changed through His all-sufficient grace and power.

*And God is able to make all grace abound to you, so that having all sufficiency in all things at all times, you may abound in every good work. II Corinthians 9:8*

*May you relish and radiate Christ!*

*Nancy W. Carroll*

# Reality Christianity: A Study of II Corinthians

## Radiating Christ in Our Cracked Lives

*Goals and Scriptural Principles in this Study*

*Through this study in II Corinthians, I pray you will:*

- ✓ *Increasingly know and love the real Christ, and relish and radiate Him.*

- ✓ *Increasingly know and love the real "you," and drop veils to reveal yourself to others.*

- ✓ *Increasingly embrace the reality that "real" ministry is through Christ's power in your brokenness and weakness.*

**II Cor. 1:1-11**        **The Reality of Suffering/The Reality of Our Comforting God**

*To understand how God allows and uses suffering to rely on Him and comfort others.*

**II Cor. 1:12-2:13**        **The Reality of Failure/The Reality of Our Faithful God**

*To say AMEN to God's faithfulness and forgiveness in the midst of our failures.*

**II Cor. 2:14-3:18**        **The Reality of Inability/The Reality of Our Covenantal God**

*To continually turn to the Lord in new covenant life and be aware of our old covenant paradigm.*

**II Cor. 4:1-5:10**        **The Reality of Cracked Pots/The Reality of Our Radiating God**

*To treasure the Treasure, not the earthly container.*

**II Cor. 5:11-6:13**        **The Reality of Brokenness/The Reality of Our Reconciling God**

*To be so compelled by the reconciling love of Christ that we will be willing to risk being a wide-open minister of reconciliation.*

**II Cor. 6:14-7:16**    **The Reality of REALationships/The Reality of Our Redeeming God**

*To long to live reverent, repentant, redeeming lives because of who we are and whose we are.*


**II Cor. 8:1-9:15**    **The Reality of Reaping/The Reality of Our Enriching God**

*To be so transformed by God's grace and indescribable gift of Jesus Christ that it overflows in a thankful, giving life that glorifies God.*


**II Cor. 10**    **The Reality of Spiritual Warfare/The Reality of Our Powerful God**

*To be aware of the mental and spiritual battle to take every thought captive and obedient to Christ.*


**II Cor. 11**    **The Reality of Deception/The Reality of Our True God**

*To know and love the real Christ, real Spirit, real Gospel and learn to discern the Real Thing.*


**II Cor. 12:1-10**    **The Reality of Weakness/The Reality of Our Sufficient God**

*To see our God-given weaknesses as a means of experiencing Christ's grace, strength, and power.*


**II Cor. 12:11-13:14**    **The Reality of "REALigion"/The Reality of Christ IN Us**

*To experience two "reality checks:" Are you sure you are a Christian? How concerned are you for others' spiritual growth?*


NancyWCarroll©2021

# BIBLIOGRAPHY AND TEACHING RESOURCES

Barnett, Paul. *The Message of 2 Corinthians: Power in Weakness* Bible Speaks Today Series (Downers Grove, Ill.: InterVarsity Press, 1988).

Dorman, Ted. *Second Corinthians* Life Change Series, Karen Lee-Thorpe, ed. (Colorado Springs, Co.: NavPress, 1996).

*ESV Study Bible, English Standard Edition* (Wheaton, Ill.: Crossway Bible, 2008).

Harris, Murray J. *Second Epistle to the Corinthians*, New International Greek Testament Commentary Series (Grand Rapids, Mich.: Eerdmans Publishing Co., 2005).

Hughes, R. Kent. *2 Corinthians: Power in Weakness* Preaching the Word Series (Wheaton, Ill: Crossway Books, 2006).

*Life Application Bible* (Grand Rapids, Mich.: Zondervan Publishing House and Wheaton, Ill.: Tyndale House Publishers, 1991).

Mears, Henrietta C. *What the Bible is All About* (Ventura, Calif.: Regal Books, 1953).

*The NIV Study Bible*, edited by Kenneth Barker, (Grand Rapids, Mich.: Zondervan Corporation, 1985).

Peterson, Eugene H. *The Message* (Colorado Springs, Co.: NavPress, 1993).

Stedman, Ray C. *Authentic Christianity* (Grand Rapids, Mich.: Discovery House Publishers, 1996).

Stevens, Paul. *2 Corinthians: Finding Strength in Weakness* (Downers Grove, Ill.: InterVarsity Press, 2001).

*Unless otherwise noted, all Scripture references are from the English Standard Version.*

# Our Theme Hymn for II Corinthians

## *Jesus I am Resting, Resting*

*Lyrics by Jean S. Pigott*

Jesus I am resting, resting
In the joy of what Thou art;
I am finding out the greatness of Thy loving heart.
Thou hast bid me gaze upon Thee,
And Thy beauty fills my soul,
For by Thy transforming power
Thou hast made me whole.

*Refrain*
*Jesus, I am resting, resting*
*In the joy of what Thou art;*
*I am finding out the greatness*
*Of Thy loving heart.*

O how great Thy loving kindness.
Vaster, broader than the sea!
O how marvelous Thy goodness,
Lavished all on me!
Yes, I rest in Thee, Beloved,
Know Thy certainty of promise,
And have made it mine.

Simply trusting Thee, Lord Jesus,
I behold Thee as Thou art,
And Thy love, so pure, so changeless,
Satisfies my heart;
Satisfies its deepest longings,
Meets supplies its every need,
Compasseth me round with blessings;
Thine is love indeed!

Ever lift Thy face upon me,
As I work and wait for Thee;
Resting 'neath Thy smile, Lord Jesus,
Earth's dark shadows flee.
Brightness of my Father's glory,
Sunshine of my Father's face,
Keep me ever trusting, resting;
Fill me with Thy grace.

# The Get REAL Club

We long for "**real**-ationships"—with God, our spouses, families, friends, and work/classmates. Our God is a relational, redemptive God who through Jesus Christ seeks us out for the ultimate Abba Father/beloved child relationship. This study gives an opportunity to be real and connect with a smaller group.

Please respect God's Word and each other as you discuss the weekly lesson. If you haven't had time to read the Scripture and think about the questions that week, please use the group discussion time to listen to other group members. The Holy Spirit is present and working and desires you as a group to experience the revelation of his truth. To be a safe group, **always maintain confidentiality with what is shared by the other members**, unless given permission to share beyond your group.

Here are some simple principles to think of as you begin connecting with your small group members in a "REAL" way.

R          <u>Be real!</u>  Be vulnerable. Let group members see the real you. (Scary, huh!)

               <u>Respect:</u> Their time, confidences, privacy, relationships.

E          <u>Encourage</u> with Christ and Scripture.

               <u>Envelop</u> with prayer.

               <u>Envision</u> who they are and what they can be in Christ.

A          <u>Available:</u> Being fully present to others is a gift.

               <u>Approachable:</u> If you let them see the real you, they'll feel safe with you.

L          <u>Look:</u> See them as Christ sees them.

               <u>Listen</u> with your heart. Don't interrupt but follow up with questions of curiosity.

               <u>Love</u> with Christ's love

# Ten Commandments for Being in a Small Group

## Thou Shalt Remember

The Lord Thy God is sovereign over what group thou are in and who thine leader is. He loves thee and will never leave nor forsake thee (Joshua 1:5-6). Remember that God worketh through His Holy Word, Holy Spirit, and holy people. Remember that it feeleth somewhat uncomfortable and artificial for everyone, especially in the beginning (see *Thou Shalt Be Patient* below.)

## Thou Shalt Respect

*The Word of God* and its supernatural living power to work in lives. If you haven't had time to do your lesson, listen more, share less.

*Time:* Come on time. End on time. Groups begin dissolving if they can't keep to the time limits.

*Each person in thine group*, personality and point of view and story. Everyone has pains, fears, sin habits, struggles, insecurities.

*Thine families and friends.* Don't share anything about anyone that you may regret later.

*Confidentiality:* What is shared in the group stays in the group unless given permission.

## Thou Shalt Be Prepared and Participate

Thou hast made a commitment to be in Scripture and walk with others in some of the significant aspects of their hearts and lives. 'Tis a privilege. Trust God that He will give thee time to prepare and courage to share and faith that thou will receive and be transformed.

## Thou Shalt Keep Focused

Keep on topic. Actively listen. Eliminate distractions. Turneth off cell phones. Thou shalt not text or start side conversations or interrupt others while they are sharing.

## Thou Shalt Repent of Fixing

'Tis not the place to fix nor give advice. 'Tis a place to listen and to focus on God's Word and be honest. We all long for a place of safety and strength where we are listened to and reminded of the gospel and pointed to Christ and Scripture.

## Thou Shalt Handle with Care

Thou shalt not gossip or judge or correct. We're all broken people in a broken world. Pray that God will give thee a supernatural love for each person in your group.

## Thou Shalt Be Patient

There will not be instant chemistry and it will take time to build trust and connect with each other.

## Thou Shalt Connect

Thou shalt pray for and connect with the other members in your group. In some groups, 'tis essential to wear nametags if only for the sake of the swiss-cheese brained among thee.

## Thou Shalt Pause

For thou who love to leapeth into each conversation and answereth each question, train thyself to pause to give non-leapers a chance to muster the courage to answer or share. Encourage others by actively listening and validating their responses through nods.

## Thou Shalt Pray

Pray without ceasing for thyself and thine group, thine leader and thine teacher and for the glory of our Triune God. Share real requests with thine group members and remember to pray for each other throughout the week.

# Personal Discovery Sheet

At the end of each weekly lesson, you are invited to complete a Personal Discovery Sheet. This gives you a way to approach a specific section of Scripture in what I call an "hour-glass" method. You begin broadly by listing the content or verses. Narrow it down to two to four main thoughts. Then funnel it into a short sentence as the main subject of the verses you are studying. Then widen back out to state the aim of the author for that passage and how to phrase that in a question. Finally, in the final section broaden to apply the passage to your life.

This approach often appeals to those who love word puzzles or, like me, are scattered and need a framework to help them organize their thoughts. This discovery sheet also helps prepare you to teach by narrowing in on the main themes and applications of a specific passage of Scripture. I've found it's wonderful when a group shares the results of their personal discovery sheets. It reveals how the Holy Spirit uses all of us together to communicate and apply his living Word.

Below is a brief description for each section. The following page is a sample from II Corinthians 4:1-5:10

# Personal Discovery Sheet

*Bible Verses*

## CONTENT

Read the passage enough times to be comfortable with contents. List the content by verse or larger section. This is usually between five to twenty concepts based on how many verses you're reading. Look for repeated phrases or words that seem to characterize the passage and include them in your list. Underline, circle, or emphasize words that seem to be the most important.

## DIVISIONS

Divide the content into two to four main "thoughts." Use a sentence as a heading for each division. Write the verses down for each division.

## ESSENCE OF PASSAGE

Using the divisions from the passage, write a ten-word or less subject sentence that gives you the thrust of the passage. Ask yourself, "What is this passage about?" Ideally, the subject sentence should be specific enough that you would be able to locate it in the Bible.

## ESSENTIAL QUESTION/AIM

The aim is the main transformational truth you want to learn, remember, or do after reading this Scripture. It may be just for yourself or include others. Ask yourself, "What do I want to remember and live by after reading this passage?" Your aim should be short and definite and should point to the hope of what God and his grace can do in and through you for his glory, not what you're going to "try harder" to do for him. Putting it in a form of a question helps to link it to applications.

## APPLICATIONS

Write specific questions or challenges based on your essential aim/question and from the divisions. Are there specific areas in which you need to repent? To believe God and his Word? To live out and apply the gospel? To see and rely on Christ? To have or communicate hope?

# OPTIONAL PERSONAL DISCOVERY SHEET

II Corinthians 4:1-5:10

## CONTENT

4:1: Therefore, by God's mercy we have this ministry do not lose heart.

4:2: We renounce shameful things and set forth God's truth plainly.

4:3-4: Gospel is veiled to perishing; unbelievers can't see the light of Christ.

4:5-6: We preach Jesus Christ as Lord and ourselves as servants, God makes light shine in our hearts to show knowledge of God in the face of Christ.

4:7: We have treasure in jars of clay to show God's all-surpassing power.

4:8-12: We are hard pressed, not crushed; struck down, not destroyed; carrying the death of Christ, so life of Christ may be revealed.

4:13-15: We hope in the resurrecting power of God and that it will benefit you and cause thankfulness to overflow to the glory of God.

4:16-18: Don't lose heart, though outwardly wasting, inwardly being daily renewed, our trials are outweighed by eternal glory. Fix eyes not on seen but eternal.

5:1-4: If earthly tent destroyed, we have eternal house in heaven and we groan for immortality.

5:5: God made us for this purpose and given us Spirit as deposit of what is to come.

5:6-8: Confident that if away from body, home with Lord. Live by faith, not sight, prefer to be with Lord.

5:9-10: Our goal is to please the Lord. We will appear before the judgment seat of Christ to receive what is due us.

## DIVISIONS

I.   II Corinthians 4:1-12: Paul reveals our purpose to radiate Christ through our jars of clay.

II.  II Corinthians 4:13-18: Paul focuses hope on resurrection, daily renewal, and eternal glory.

III. II Corinthians 5:1-10: Paul describes his longing for heaven and his goal of pleasing the Lord.

## ESSENCE OF PASSAGE

Paul refocuses Corinthians on Treasure, eternity in this temporal life.

## ESSENTIAL QUESTION/AIM

How will I treasure the Treasure and not focus so much on my earthly container?

## APPLICATIONS

- How do I lose heart and what does that show about where my focus is?

- How do I communicate the Gospel to veiled minds?

- What is more important to me, the Treasure or the container?

- How can I more and more have an eternal perspective? Where am I focused on what's seen or temporary?

- What do I long for? Where is my home? What is my goal?

# Suggestions for Doing Weekly Lessons

## Warning! Life Change Ahead.

You are entering supernatural territory. Through God's Holy Word, Holy Spirit and holy people, your life will be changed. Please take this study seriously. Give yourself the time and space to invite the Holy Spirit to be with you as you read and meditate on these daily Scriptures. Approach Scriptures as God's love letter to you and trust His Spirit to guide you. Train yourself to go the primary source, the Bible, before reading commentary.

## Your Daily Time with God

This Bible study uses Head/Heart/Hand questions for studying, believing, and applying Scripture. We pray that God's Word would work through your head (your intellect, what you think and believe), your heart (your inner being, what you feel, how you respond), and your hands (what flows out of your life in response to what you think, believe, and feel). For those whose "reality" is that you hunger to be in God's Word but are continually frustrated by the lack of time, we have created a "Bible Study Express" approach which allows you to do the lesson more quickly by just answering the questions with an asterick (*).

## Personal Discovery Sheet

At the end of each weekly lesson is an optional discovery sheet. It is a different way to engage deeply with Scripture and meditate on the essence of a passage and how it applies to your life. Try it out to see if this approach helps embed Scripture into your soul and relationships.

## Small Group Time and Prayer Time

If you are part of a small group doing this study, we pray your group develops into a place of safe, growing, and loving community. During the group discussion, if you haven't had time to complete the lesson, try to speak less and listen more. You'll find a prayer journal at the back of the book so that you can write down and remember to pray for yourself and one another through the weeks of this study.

# Week 1: What is Real?
## Overview of II Corinthians

*Questions marked with an \* are for those doing "Bible Study Express."*

 **Scan II Corinthians.** (Look over outline of book, subheads, repeated words or phrases, verses that "jump" out for you.) What are some of the major themes of the book? What repeated words or phrases do you find?

**Extra:** Reading through the entire book in one sitting helps you better understand the author's main purpose. Carve out about an hour to read through II Corinthians.

*"What is real?"* asked the Velveteen Rabbit. The Skin Horse said, *"Real isn't how you are made, it is a thing that happens when you are loved for a long, long time. Generally, by the time you are real most of your hair has been loved off, and your eyes drop out and you get loose in the joints and very shabby. But these things don't matter at all, because once you are REAL you can't be ugly except to those who don't understand. Once you are real you can't become unreal again. It lasts for always."*

Margery Williams, *The Velveteen Rabbit*

What does it mean to "be real?" Give an example.

Pause for a moment and think about how you want God to make himself more real to you this year and how you want to "radiate" Christ to those around you. Write down one or two personal goals for this study.*

**Scan II Corinthians.** This is Paul's most personal letter to a church he planted, loved, and confronted. Most of Paul's epistles begin with doctrinal truths of who we are in Christ and end with exhortations on how to live out of that identity. II Corinthians is different in that Paul is revealing what a real Christian ministry looks like through exposing his own suffering and weaknesses, and who Jesus Christ is in the midst of his reality (II Corinthians 4:6).

One of Paul's realities was defending himself to those he helped lead to the Lord. The Corinthians were being enticed away from Paul by "super apostles," the ancient equivalent of slick television evangelists or "health and wealth" preachers.

Write down your observations about what a real minister and real ministry of the gospel is.

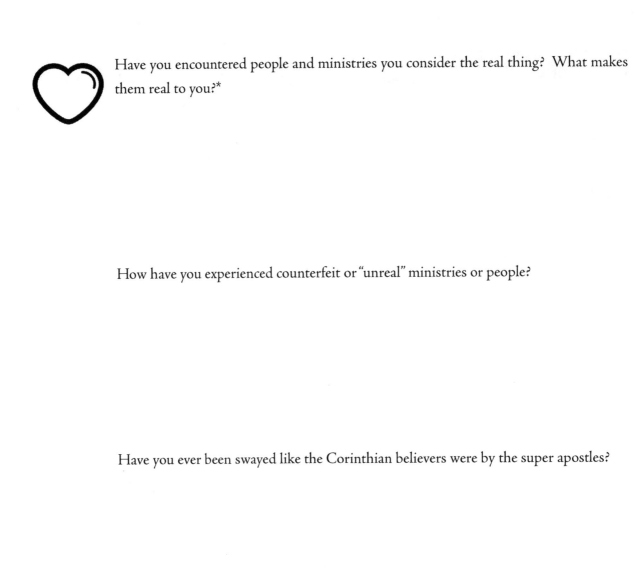

Have you encountered people and ministries you consider the real thing? What makes them real to you?*

How have you experienced counterfeit or "unreal" ministries or people?

Have you ever been swayed like the Corinthian believers were by the super apostles?

What was the result?

Where are you right now—radiating realities through your cracks (II Corinthians 4:7) or hiding behind veils (II Corinthians 3:14)?*

Pray that God will reveal areas in your life where you may be hiding behind veils or masks. Ask your group to pray for you to drop some of your masks during this study.

**Read II Corinthians 1:3-7, 13:11-14.** Paul begins and ends his letter with *comfort*. What is comfort?

Why does Paul emphasize comfort? Why do we need it?

**Stop scanning and start meditating:** Write down how we can receive and give comfort through these verses in II Corinthians:

**1:9**

**1:20-22**

**2:14-15**

3:4-6


3:11-18


4:6-7


4:16-17


5:14-21


8:9


9:8


12:9-10

Which of these verses above give you the most comfort and hope?* Why?

 *God's grace is sufficient in our weakness.* Write down areas where you need God's grace and power in this season of your life.* Ask your group to pray for you.

**Read II Corinthians 9:6-8.** What truth does Paul share in verse 6?* How have you experienced this truth?

What is God able to do according to verse 8?*

How many times does Paul say "all" and "every" in verse 8? Does he leave out anything?

Meditate on the promise found in II Corinthians 9:8. Where do you not believe God will give you all the grace you need?

To what "good work" do you think God is calling you where you will need his abounding grace?

 This study will take commitment to sowing Scripture into your soul daily and sharing it with your group weekly. Will you commit to making this study a priority in the demands of life? Ask God to enable you to be in Scripture consistently.* Ask your group to keep you accountable.

Write down one or two specific things you want to reap from this study and one or two ways you hope to reach out to others in abounding grace.*

# *Week 1: What is Real?*
## Overview of II Corinthians

*"What is real?" asked the Velveteen Rabbit. The Skin Horse said, "Real isn't how you are made, it is a thing that happens when you are loved for a long, long time. Generally, by the time you are real most of your hair has been loved off, and your eyes drop out and you get loose in the joints and very shabby. But these things don't matter at all, because once you are REAL you can't be ugly except to those who don't understand. Once you are real you can't become unreal again. It lasts for always."*

Margery Williams, *The Velveteen Rabbit* (New York: Simon & Schuster, 1975).

## GROUP DISCUSSION

✓ *Think about a person you know who is the "real thing." What makes them real to you? What attracts you and what scares you about being that real?*

## TEACHING TIME

✓ WHY ARE WE STUDYING THE BIBLE?

R

E

A

L

✓ WHY ARE WE STUDYING II CORINTHIANS?

✓ WHAT IS II CORINTHIANS ABOUT?

✓ GOALS FOR THIS STUDY

## REALITY CHECK

*Do you feel real in your relationship with Christ? With others? With yourself? Why or why not?*

*Talk to Christ honestly about your own "reality," your longings and loneliness. Listen for his loving reply.*

## REAL REALITY: SCRIPTURE MEDITATION

*BELIEVE IT. IT'S TRUE, AND TRUE FOR YOU.*

*And God is able to make all grace abound to you, so that in all things at all times, having all that you need, you will abound in every good work.*
*II Corinthians 9:8*

# Reality Christianity:
# Radiating Christ in Our Cracked Lives

## Week 1: Overview of II Corinthians

*What is Real?*

## Why Are We Studying II Corinthians?

In the epistle to the Romans, Paul clearly lays out Gospel 101. In II Corinthians, he leaps to a graduate level, Gospel 301, as he reveals how the Christian life is lived out in relationships. It is Paul's most vulnerable letter to some of his most difficult spiritual children, the Corinthians. "This book is about the nature of the gospel and authentic ministry. Those who really care about the gospel and the care of souls will find II Corinthians captivating. For those who don't care, this is about where your heart should be—and what you ought to be about."[1] As you embrace God's truth to you in II Corinthians, you will be relieved that authentic Christian living is not based on your competence or strength, but on God's grace and power (II Cor. 3:5, 12:9). You will grapple with the glorious mystery of living a new covenant life that is not based on the formulas or rules of the old covenant (II Cor. 3), but on a living, vital relationship with Jesus Christ, where real Christian ministry means dropping veils to reveal his glory (II Cor. 3:16), trusting Christ to use our broken jars of clay (II Cor. 4:7), and allowing the Spirit to give us life, freedom, and transformation into Christ's image (II Cor. 3:4-18). We are studying II Corinthians so we can relish and radiate Christ in our cracked lives (II Cor. 4:6-7) for God's glory, for our hope, and for those who will gain hope from seeing Christ shining through our lives. The 13-week journey will be filled with hard realities of suffering, failures, inabilities, and brokenness juxtaposed with holy realities of God's compassion, faithfulness, ability, and reconciliation. This "reality series" will be worth it as we end with Paul praising our Triune God, "The grace of our Lord Jesus Christ and the love of God and the fellowship of the Holy Spirit be with you all." (II Cor. 13:14)

## Where Do We Begin?  An Overview of II Corinthians

Who is Paul?  What's going on in his life at this point? The author, the Apostle Paul, is at a critical point of his ministry, forced to defend himself and his ministry to his own spiritual children against the "super apostles" (II Cor. 11). This epistle is "Paul's major defense of his apostleship to his detractors."[2]  Paul was unlike the other 11 apostles who had been with Jesus through his earthly ministry. His dramatic conversion and call to ministry came in the middle of his zealous, murderous persecution of Christians

---

1 R. Kent Hughes, *2 Corinthians: Power in Weakness* (Crossway Books: Wheaton, IL, 2006), 15.

2 Paul Barnett, *The Message of 2 Corinthians* (Inter-Varsity Press:  Downers Grove, IL, 1988), 17.

(Acts 9). Jesus radically chose Saul, the "Jew's Jew" to minister to the Gentiles as well as to kings and the children of Israel and to suffer for his name's sake (Acts 9:15-16). Everything changed, even his name, now Paul, "little one." He wrote II Corinthians in AD 55-56 from Macedonia during his third missionary journey about 18 months after he addressed multiple church problems in I Corinthians. This epistle should be called "Fourth" Corinthians as two "painful" letters to the Corinthians (see I Cor. 5:9, II Cor. 2:3-4) have been lost, one preceding I Corinthians and one preceding II Corinthians. In this "most emotional of all the apostle's writings"[3] Paul reveals, "his injured love, of paradoxically wounded, relentless affection"[4] for his people while he glories in the gospel and embraces God's strength in his weakness. Paul's words and life call the Corinthians and us to be real in our Christianity and radiate Christ's light and power amidst our brokenness.

**Who were these Corinthians?** "When Paul visited Corinthian in AD 49-50, the city was just over 80 years old with a population of some 80,000. Yet, during its short history Corinth had become the third most important city of the Roman Empire behind Alexandria and Rome itself."[5] It was a wild and worldly city situated at the crossroads of trade between the Aegean and Ionian Seas. Most of the Corinthians were Gentiles, freedmen (former slaves), and slaves. Scott Hafemann notes, "Corinth was a free-wheeling 'boom town,' filled with materialism, pride and the self-confidence that comes with having made it in a new place and with a new social identity. The 'pull-yourself-up-by-your-bootstraps' mentality that would become so characteristic of the American frontier filled the air."[6] The "theology of weakness and suffering was foolish in new Corinth with its worship of self-made wealth and power."[7]

**What are some central themes of the book?** Chapters 1-7 show what it's like to be a real, faithful, new covenant Christian. Chapters 8-9 show what it's like to be a repentant and grateful Christian. Chapters 10-13 is a reality check to those who are not repentant. The overall theme of being a real Christian in a real world is captured in Christ's response to Paul's pleas for release from his 'thorn' in II Cor. 12:9: "My grace is sufficient for you, for my power is made perfect in weakness." II Corinthians reveals Jesus Christ as the All Sufficient One who provides his power and grace as we walk out our faith in a fallen world. As we turn our eyes to the face of Jesus Christ, we will reflect the glory of God (II Cor. 4:6). My prayer is that we relish and radiate Christ together in our cracked lives!

---

3 Hughes, 15.

4 Ibid, 15.

5 Hughes, 13. Quoting Scott J. Hafemann.

6 Quoted in Hughes, 14.

7 Hughes, 20.

# Week 2: The Reality of Suffering
## II Corinthians 1:1-11

*Questions marked with an * are for those doing "Bible Study Express."*

 **Read II Corinthians 1:1-11.** What facts about the author Paul do you find in these opening verses?*

What is your first impression of Paul?*

**Read Acts 9:1-22 and Philippians 3:3-11** to learn more about Paul (called Saul at the time) before and after his dramatic conversion and call to serve God. What was Paul like before God grabbed him?

How did he change after his conversion?

In Acts 9:15-16 what does God call Paul to do for him?

To whom does God send Paul?

What does God show him?

 Few have as dramatic an encounter with God as Paul did. But we all must connect with God in a real and personal way. How has God grabbed your heart and life?*

How has God surprised you by taking you to places and people not in your "plans" or comfort zone?

 Paul begins II Corinthians with: *Grace to you and peace from God our Father and the Lord Jesus Christ* (verse 1:2). It is how he begins most of his letters and is more than just a greeting. It is his heart for his "people." Meditate on this verse today, asking for his grace and peace in your life. Ask the Holy Spirit to make you aware of his grace and peace as you consider God as Father and Jesus Christ as Lord.

Consolidate the message of II Corinthians 1:1-11 into one sentence. Share that sentence with a family member, friend, or someone in your group this week.*

*Optional: Do discovery sheet on II Corinthians 1:1-11 found at end of the weekly lesson.*

*"In I Corinthians Paul lets us see inside a first-century church. But in II Corinthians Paul lets us see inside a first-century Christian, the apostle himself."*

Paul Stevens

**Read Acts 18:1-17.** Paul visited Corinth on his second missionary journey (AD 48-50) and wrote II Corinthians in Macedonia about AD 56. Greece's major trading center, Corinth was a wealthy and wild city housing the Temple of Aphrodite. Skim through I and II Corinthians (look at basic outlines of the books, subheads, major themes) to get a sense of the troubles Paul was addressing.

Write down some of the problems Paul addresses in II Corinthians.*

From your quick review, what do you think Corinth was like?

Do you feel like you live in a "Corinth?" What kind of problems or troubles are you facing?

Do most of these troubles or discomforts occur in your family, church, community, work, school, or inside yourself?

Which problem that Paul addresses in II Corinthians do you most need God to help you deal with as you go through this study?*

**Read II Corinthians 1:1-11.** Paul touches on one of the themes of II Corinthians in these opening verses. Looking at verses 1:3-7, what is one theme Paul emphasizes?*

How does the suffering of Christ relate to the comfort of Christ?

From these verses, does God promise to deliver us from trials, troubles, and sufferings?

What does he promise?*

What is Paul's hope (verse 7)?

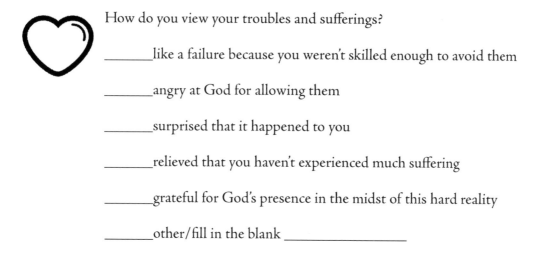

How do you view your troubles and sufferings?

_____like a failure because you weren't skilled enough to avoid them

_____angry at God for allowing them

_____surprised that it happened to you

_____relieved that you haven't experienced much suffering

_____grateful for God's presence in the midst of this hard reality

_____other/fill in the blank _____

These difficult verses on suffering often stay stuck in our heads. How do you get biblical truth about suffering from your head to your heart? How can you trust that God is the Father of mercies and comfort in the midst of your suffering?*

Think about times of suffering or trouble you have experienced and how you viewed or related to God about them. Write how you responded to God and the situation. Re-read verses 1-11 and write a biblical response (not a "religious" one!) to God and suffering.

**Read II Corinthians 1:1-11.** Paul opens II Corinthians with praise. List the attributes of God and Jesus Christ you see in these verses.*

Comfort comes from the Greek *parakaleo* which means to come alongside. Other related words are *encourage, exhort, console, counsel, and advocate.* What aspect of comfort do you see in the following verses?

Psalm 23:4

Jeremiah 31:12-14

Matthew 5:4

Jesus uses the word *paraklesis* (comforter or counselor) when speaking of the Holy Spirit. From these verses, what does Jesus promise that the Holy Spirit will do for and in you?

John 14:15-20

John 14:25-27

John 16:5-15

Have you ever been comforted or tried to comfort someone in a way that seemed to make the situation worse? What made it ineffective or more painful?

Have you ever received real comfort from God or from one of his people? Describe ways that you have been comforted in your sufferings or troubles.*

 How will you comfort others with the comfort God has given you? Write down specific areas where you have received comfort in your affliction where you can comfort someone else.

Pray for a spirit of forgiveness for those who have tried to comfort you but just added to the pain. Pray for awareness and repentance of ways you may have caused pain when you've tried to comfort someone.

## Day 5: Real Hope

**Read II Corinthians 1:9-11.** What lesson in verse 9 did Paul learn that he wants us to learn as well?*

Where is Paul's hope set? (verses 7, 10)?*

Why is the resurrection so closely tied to hope?

What help is Paul asking for (verse 10) and what response is he confident of (verse 11)?

As you think of some of the difficulties you are facing, who are you relying on to fix it or bear with it?*

 Don't miss Paul's emphasis on the importance and need for prayer. Write down where you need prayer and share it with your group.*

Take the commitment of praying for others seriously. Use the *Personal and Group Prayer Journal* section at the end of this study to keep track of specific prayer requests you've received from your group and pray this week!

# OPTIONAL PERSONAL DISCOVERY SHEET

II Corinthians 1:1-11

## CONTENT

List the main points from this Scripture.

## DIVISIONS

Divide content into 2-4 main sections and write a sentence for each division.

## ESSENCE OF PASSAGE

Write a short sentence (10 words or less!) that gives the thrust of the passage.

## ESSENTIAL QUESTION/AIM

Write the main "transformational truth" to remember from studying this Scripture. Make this as short and simple as possible. It helps to put it in the form of a question to link it to application.

## APPLICATIONS

Write specific questions or challenges to help put the aim into action or answer the question. Are there specific areas in which you need to repent? To believe God and his Word? To live out and apply the gospel?

# *Week 2: The Reality of Suffering*
# II Corinthians 1:1-11

## GROUP DISCUSSION

- ✓ How have *you reacted to suffering in your own life?*

- ✓ *How have you relied on God in your suffering?*

## TEACHING TIME

### THE REALITY OF PAUL'S LIFE: II Corinthians 1:1-2

### THE REALITY OF SUFFERING: II Corinthians 1:3-7

- RELISH GOD'S ATTRIBUTES

- RETHINK COMFORT

- RETHINK SUFFERING

### WRONG THINKING:

- *LACK OF SUFFERING IS AN AMERICAN OR CHRISTIAN RIGHT.*

- *IT'S ALL MY FAULT (OR ALL THEIR FAULT).*

### RIGHT THINKING:

- *SUFFERING HAPPENS.*

- *GOD ALLOWS SUFFERING FOR HIS GLORY, OUR GOOD.*
  - You will know and rely on God more.
  - You will long for your true home.
  - You will minister to others in their suffering.

# THE REALITY OF OUR RESURRECTING GOD: II CORINTHIANS 1:8-11

## WRONG THINKING

- Co-pilot syndrome

- Free-ticket syndrome

## RIGHT THINKING

- New "Real"ationship

- Relying on continuous deliverance

- Suffering is not a solo sport. Suffering as a community.

## RESPONSE

How will you choose to respond to suffering?

# REALITY CHECK

✓ *Since suffering is a "reality," how can you suffer well? In the midst of your suffering, how can you experience God's comfort and give it to others?*

# REAL REALITY: SCRIPTURE MEDITATION

*BELIEVE IT. IT'S TRUE, AND TRUE FOR YOU.*
*Blessed be the God and Father of our Lord Jesus Christ, the Father of mercies and God of all comfort, who comforts us in all our affliction, so that we may be able to comfort those who are in any affliction, with the comfort with which we ourselves are comforted by God.  II Cor. 1:3-4*

*Indeed, we felt that we had received the sentence of death. But that was to make us rely not on ourselves but on God who raises the dead. He delivered us from such a deadly peril, and he will deliver us. On him we have set our hope that he will deliver us again. II Corinthians 1:9-10*

# Reality Christianity:
# Radiating Christ in Our Cracked Lives

## Week 2: II Corinthians 1:1-11

*The Reality of Suffering / The Reality of our Comforting God*


## Paul: Proving His Ministry is the Real Thing
## II Corinthians 1:1-2

Paul, the founder of the Corinthian Church, humbles himself to prove to his own spiritual children that he was an apostle of Christ Jesus by the will of God (vs. 1). "Apostle (*apostolos*) emphasizes that Paul's authority is equal to that of the 12 apostles chosen by Christ. The apostles were specifically called by Christ and had seen the risen Lord Jesus. They established and governed the whole church, under Jesus Christ, and they had authority to speak and write the words of God, equal in authority to the OT Scriptures. Paul was called to be an apostle when Jesus appeared to him on the Damascus road (Acts 9; 22; 26), and the unusual timing of his call led Paul to conclude that no more apostles would be chosen after him (1 Cor. 15:8)."[8] It is a bold word spoken with humility and authority. Paul was "commissioned directly by Christ for permanent and distinctive leadership in the universal church."[9] He directs this letter to the church at Corinth and more broadly to the region of Achaia. Be encouraged that although the Corinthians struggled with sin, Paul saw them as saints (holy ones). "The Bible speaks of saints as quite ordinary people whom God graciously regards as special to him through their faith-commitment to his Son Jesus. Moreover, God not only treats believers as holy, he actively makes them so by the dynamic presence of the Holy Spirit in the inner recesses of their lives, conforming them to the pattern of Christ."[10] Grace and peace is more than a same-old salutation. Paul's greeting of **grace** (charis: God's **R**iches at **C**hrist's **E**xpense II Cor. 8:9, his unmerited favor) and **peace** (shalom: wholeness, "not untroubled circumstances but the profound well-being that comes from resting in God's sovereignty and mercy."[11]) sets the book's theme of reconciliation in our brokenness and need.

---

8 *ESV Study Bible*, Notes on Romans 1:1

9 Murray J. Harris, *The Second Epistle to the Corinthians* (Eerdmans Publishing Co: Grand Rapids, MI, 2005), 128.

10 Paul Barnett, *The Message of 2 Corinthians* (Inter-Varsity Press: Downers Grove, IL, 1988), 27.

11 *ESV Study Bible*, Notes on II Corinthians 1:2.

## The Reality of Suffering/The Reality of our Comforting God
## II Corinthians 1:3-7

View this section as a doxology (hymn of praise) to God whose attributes shine through the reality of our suffering. Paul identifies God as Father to the Lord Jesus Christ so there is no doubt He is Father "only as they acknowledge Jesus to be God's Son and their Lord. . . to reject Jesus as Lord would be to repudiate God as Father."[12] Jesus is equally God. Paul shows God in relationship to us as our Father who is full of compassion and comfort. This is the God found in Isaiah 40-66 who comforts as a mother (Isa. 66:13) and prophesizes a Messianic comforter that is confirmed in Jesus as the *consolation of Israel* (Luke 2:25). "It was and is through Christ that the comfort of God the Father comes."[13] Suffering in all its forms appears 17 times in these five verses. **Comfort** (*parakaleo*) appears ten times and means to come alongside, to strengthen, to be present with, to embolden in belief or course of action.[14] It is also one of the primary names of the Holy Spirit (*parakletes*) as the one who intercedes, mediates, helps. How do we humbly approach the subject of suffering, especially to those who have suffered the most? Honestly. Biblically. Even hopefully, for there is purpose in suffering for the believer.

Suffering should not be a surprise or a guilt trip that you didn't try hard enough to avoid it. It is reality, especially to those committed fully to Christ. George MacDonald says, "The Son of God suffered unto the death, not that men might not suffer, but that their suffering might be like His."[15] Take comfort in the God who suffered as he sent his own Son to die for us (Jn. 3:16, Rom. 5:8). "In Jesus Christ, God experienced the greatest depth of pain. Therefore, though Christianity does not provide the reason for each experience of pain, it provides deep resources for facing suffering with hope and courage rather than bitterness and despair. . .if we embrace that Jesus is God and that he went to the Cross, then we have deep consolation and strength to face the brutal realities of life on earth. We can know that God is truly *Immanuel*—God *with* us—even in our worst sufferings."[16] Suffering is not a solo sport. God calls us to comfort others (come alongside) with the comfort we have received from him and to pray for one another (vs. 11).

## The Reality of Relying on our Resurrecting God
## II Corinthians 1:8-11

Paul reveals his desperation to the Corinthians. Eugene Peterson in *The Message*, translates vs. 9-10, "It was so bad we didn't think we were going to make it. We felt like we'd been sent to death row, that it was

---

12  Barnett, 29.

13  R. Kent Hughes, *2 Corinthians: Power in Weakness* (Crossway Books: Wheaton, IL, 2006), 23.

14  Frederick Danker and Walter Bauer, *BDAG 3rd ed* (University of Chicago Press: Chicago, 2000), 764.

15  Hughes, 25.

16  Timothy Keller, *The Reason for God* (Riverhead Books: New York, 2008) 28, 31.

all over for us. As it turned out, it was the best thing that could have happened. Instead of trusting in our own strength or wits to get out of it, *we were forced to trust God totally*—not a bad idea since he's the God who raises the dead! And he did it, rescued us from certain doom. And he'll do it again, rescuing us as many times as we need rescuing." Have you ever been there? It feels like you're giving up. That you will die. That you are *forced to trust God totally*. We prefer to live like God is our co-pilot or the giver of the "golden ticket" to safe and happy salvation. He promises resurrection and ongoing deliverance (past, present, future) amid the despair and death and nightmares of our times of suffering. Note the tenses Paul uses in describing God: "The God on whom Paul relied was the living God, the God who continues to act now. He was not only the God 'who raised the Lord Jesus' (past tense) and who 'will...raise us' (future tense) (4:14, 5:15), he is also the God who *continues to raise the dead* (present tense)."[17] He is the God who has, who will, and who is now delivering you in your troubles. "This is the endless refrain that comes to all committed believers—God by nature is the Deliverer, Redeemer, and Savior who raises the dead."[18] Paul exposes the reality of a minister of the gospel. "Affliction—death—resurrection is the central law of life and ministry as affliction draws you down to the end of yourself ('death') and then you look to Christ, finding yourself thrust upward in resurrection for further ministry. . .Christ's call to take up the cross and follow him is nothing less than a call to embrace this cycle."[19] Suffering is a reality. The choice is yours on how you respond or whom you rely on. "If God is to become our home, our place of rest in the midst of grief no human can cure, then the channel must be narrowed. We must come to the point when we realize that God is our only full comforter, our only true healer."[20] Gerald Sittser writing of losing his wife, mother, and young daughter in *A Grief Disguised*, points out, "Never have I felt so broken; yet never have I felt so whole. Never have I been so aware of my weakness and vulnerability; yet never have been more content and so strong. . . what I considered mutually exclusive—sorrow and joy, pain and pleasure, death and life—have become parts of a greater whole." God is our Comforting and Compassionate Father, our Reliable Deliverer and Resurrection in all our suffering. Are you willing to relinquish and rely on him alone?

---

17  Barnett, 34.

18  Hughes, 33.

19  Hughes, 32.

20  Sally Breedlove, *Choosing Rest: Cultivating a Sunday Heart in a Monday World* (NavPress: Colorado Springs, CO., 2002), 117.

# Week 3: The Reality of Failure
## II Corinthians 1:12-2:13

*Questions marked with an \* are for those doing "Bible Study Express."*

## Day 1: The Reality of Our Inconsistency

**Read II Corinthians 1:12-2:13.** What kind of criticism is Paul is addressing from the Corinthians?*

In changing his plans because of circumstances out of his control, Paul never changes his main objective in relation to the church of Corinth. What is Paul's main goal with the church according to these verses?

Have you ever had to change your plans after saying you would do something? How did it make you feel?

What did others say?

How do you handle the failures and inconsistencies in your own life and the lives of those around you (especially your spouse, children, parents, leaders, friends)?*

 *In me, no guarantees. In Christ, always yes.* Where have you tried to be the "yes" to someone (your child, spouse, close friend) instead of pointing them to Christ?

Ask God to trust in what Christ can do in their lives and courage to turn their eyes upon Jesus.

Consolidate the message of II Corinthians 1:12-2:13 into one sentence. Share that sentence with a family member, friend, or someone in your group this week.

*Optional: Do discovery sheet on II Corinthians 1:12-2:13 found at the end of this weekly lesson.*

**Read II Corinthians 1:12-2:4.** Write down the attributes of God, Jesus Christ, and the Holy Spirit you find in this passage.*

GOD:

JESUS CHRIST:

HOLY SPIRIT:

What evidence in verses 18-22 does Paul give of God's "always yes" in Christ?

What part of that is most meaningful to you right now?

If you are confused because you seem to be hearing "no!" from God, pray honestly and ask God to reveal Himself to you as your faithful, promise-keeping God in a real way this week.*

Ask Him to reassure you that He is making you stand firm in Christ and He has sealed you for His own and loves you.

 Paul redirects the believers from their own failures to God's faithfulness through Jesus Christ. To encourage your heart, write down biblical promises where you have experienced God's "yes in Christ" and share with your group.*

**Read II Corinthians 1:23-2:4.** What are some of the emotions Paul feels for the Corinthian believers?*

What does this show of Paul's character and his investment in the Corinthian believers?

How much are you willing to risk in your relationships?*

In your longing for "real" relationships, are you willing to work through pain, grief, and disappointment to reach deeper joy and love?

How willing are you to bring up hard issues, cause "good grief," and be vulnerable to those in your closer circles (your family, friends, co-workers, church members, others)? Describe times you have entered more vulnerably into relationships and what the result was.

 Are you someone who avoids conflict and hard truth, or do you tend to jump in too quickly to confront?

Pray for the Holy Spirit to give you a deep love and courage to be in deeper relationships with others.*

**Read II Corinthians 2:5-11.** Also read I Corinthians 5:1-5 (possibly referring to the same situation) and Matthew 18:15-17. What are some of the principles of discipline and forgiveness found in these verses?*

What should be the main goal of discipline?*

What are Satan's schemes, according to the II Corinthian verses and I Peter 5:6-11?

When do you have trouble believing the promise of God to forgive and restore you in Christ Jesus?

If someone has hurt you, how far do they have to go earn the "right" to be restored?*

How passionate are you for the unity and purity of the church? Are you passionate enough to get involved in other people's lives in difficult situations?

Write down where you need to lovingly confront and also where you need to forgive someone.* Ask God for wisdom and courage to seek restoration.

**Read II Corinthians 1:23-2:4 and 2:12-17.** Why did Paul leave Troas despite the open door of ministry?*

From these verses, was Paul's heart with his plans or with people?  Why do you say so?

What was Paul's attitude (vs. 14) in all the changes that occurred in his journey?*

How difficult is it to let go of your agenda or plan?

As you look forward in your life (or even this week!), do you seek God in your plans?*

As you look back on your life (or your week) and the detours, delays and unexpected changes, can you see God's sovereign hand in where your life has gone?*

How can you trust him more with your past, present, and future?

Open your planner or calendar and ask God to give you eyes to see people as more than distractions or detours on your "TO DO" list.*

Ask God to give you a flexible and sensitive spirit to His will that is willing to change if He directs or you don't have peace.

# OPTIONAL PERSONAL DISCOVERY SHEET

II Corinthians 1:12-2:13

## CONTENT

List the main points from this Scripture.

## DIVISIONS

Divide content into 2-4 main sections and write a sentence for each division.

## ESSENCE OF PASSAGE

Write a short sentence (10 words or less!) that gives the thrust of the passage.

## ESSENTIAL QUESTION/AIM

Write the main "transformational truth" to remember from studying this Scripture. Make this as short and simple as possible. It helps to put it in the form of a question to link it to application.

## APPLICATIONS

Write specific questions or challenges to help put the aim into action or answer the question. Are there specific areas in which you need to repent? To believe God and his Word? To live out and apply the gospel?

# *Week 3: The Reality of Failure*
# II Corinthians 1:12-2:13

## GROUP DISCUSSION

✓ How do you react to failure in your life and others' lives?

## TEACHING TIME

### REPENT OF YOUR RESPONSE TO YOUR REALITY

*Examine Paul's response to his "reality" and your response in similar situations:*

*Failure/Lack of Control/Inconsistency*

*Criticism/Slander/Conflict*

*Sin*

### BELIEVE IN GOD'S REALITY

*How does God reveal Himself to us in this passage?*

*Faithful*

*Always Yes in Christ*

*Establisher*

*Anointer*

*Sealer/Owner*

*Guarantee in Holy Spirit*

*Forgiver/Restorer*

## FIGHT TO BELIEVE AND LIVE IN YOUR NEW REALITY

*Who are you and what does God promise you in this passage?*

*SCRIPTURE*

*Will God come through for me?* _____

*Will I fail?* _____

*Do I have a purpose? Will God use me?* _____

*Who am I? Do I belong anywhere?* _____

*Is it worth it? What's it all for?* _____

*How can I experience grief and joy at the same time?* _____

*Can I experience deep, real relationships?* _____

*Can I be forgiven and restored?* _____

*Can I be a forgiver and restorer to those who have hurt me?* _____

*How can I glorify God in the middle of my "reality?"* _____

### DO YOU BELIEVE IT?

*I am going to make it.*
*I am special to God and will be used for His Kingdom.*
*I am not my own and it's not about me and that's a good thing.*
*I am not home, but I will get there.*
*I am forgiven and restored.*

## REALITY CHECK

*Where is your biggest struggle to believe? Is it believing who God is or believing who you are in Christ? How will you fight to believe and respond differently this week?*

## REAL REALITY: SCRIPTURE MEDITATION

### BELIEVE IT. IT'S TRUE, AND TRUE FOR YOU. AMEN!

*For no matter how many promises God has made, they are "Yes" in Christ. And so through him the "Amen" is spoken by us to the glory of God. Now it is God who makes both us and you stand firm in Christ. He anointed us, set his seal of ownership on us, and put his Spirit in our hearts as a deposit, guaranteeing what is to come. II Corinthians 1:20-22.*

# Reality Christianity:
# Radiating Christ in Our Cracked Lives
## Week 3: II Corinthians 1:12-2:13
*The Reality of Failure / The Reality of our Faithful God*

## *Love* is a Verb.  *Fail* is a Noun.

In II Corinthians, Paul lives out agape love to the Corinthians, who like spiritual teenagers, seem to be shouting "What a Fail!" to Paul in light of his change of plans to come see them. "In I Corinthians Paul lets us see inside a first-century church. But in II Corinthians Paul lets us see inside a first-century Christian, the apostle himself. Through his large heart we see into the heart of God and the heart of the Christian message."[21] Paul *agapes* his people amid conflict and criticism, failure and disappointment. He chooses to be vulnerable (2:4) when accused of vacillating (1:17). He chooses not to be the people-pleasing "Yes Man" but to point to Jesus Christ as the only YES (1:20). He chooses to forgive and restore and bring the Corinthians with him on this difficult journey (2:5-11). In the midst of his own tears and anguish, he fights for their joy and faith (1:24) and glorifies the Triune God (1:20-22). He is a role model of Christian leadership.

Where are you on your spiritual journey? Are you one of the criticizing Corinthians? Are you trying to figure out how to keep on loving and looking to Christ in the midst of disappointments and failures? Are you wondering if you're a 'fail' at real Christian ministry because how hurt you are by those you're trying to lead or who are leading you? Welcome to the real world and welcome to the real Word that refocuses you on the true reality in II Corinthians 1:20-22: *For all the promises of God find their Yes in him. That is why it is through him that we utter our Amen to God for his glory. And it is God who establishes us with you in Christ, and has anointed us, and who has also put his seal on us and given us his Spirit in our hearts as a guarantee.*

## Does Anyone Live Plan A?
## II Corinthians 1:12-17, 2:12-13

Paul's *goals* for the Corinthians of loving them, working for their joy, and building them up in their faith never changed. His *plans* did. Not once, but at least twice. In Plan A (I Cor. 16:2-8), Paul's itinerary was Ephesus to Macedonia to Corinth to Jerusalem. Plan B had Paul going from Ephesus to Corinth (after

---

21 Paul Stevens, 2 Corinthians: Finding Strength in Weakness (InterVarsity Press: Downers Grove, IL, 2001) 5.

Timothy's report of rebellion in the ranks) for the "painful" visit (2:1) to Macedonia and back to Corinth. Plan "Reality" has Paul visiting Corinth to deal directly with the divisiveness created by his opponents, returning to Ephesus, from where he sent Titus with the now-lost "severe" letter. Paul travels to Troas (2:12) where he has an open door of ministry but leaves for Macedonia because he is worrying about Titus and the response to his letter (2:13). Titus brings back the good news/bad news. Paul rejoices over the majority's repentance (7:5-16) and warns against the influential rebellious minority (11:12-21). He writes II Corinthians after hearing Titus' report. Did this make Paul look like a vacillating fool to many? Yes. "Plan A was nullified when he crossed from Ephesus to Corinth on the 'painful visit,' and Plan B was nullified when he returned to Ephesus after that visit. Then he readopted Plan A, traveling from Ephesus to Macedonia to Corinth. That is, to Plan A Paul had said 'Yes-No-Yes'; to Plan B 'Yes-No.' Here was ample ammunition for his detractors' attack!"[22]

## What Will You Say Amen To?
## II Corinthians 1:20-22

Paul's defense is his conscience and sincere behavior (1:12), his desire to show mercy and spare their feelings (1:23), his working for their joy and faith (1:24), and the depth of his love for them (2:4). Paul turns their eyes to the Triune God, to the only real YES in a "no-maybe-no" world. In his anguished emotions, he points away from himself to Jesus Christ as the YES to all of God's promises (1:20-22). God is the faithful one (1:18) who establishes us in Jesus Christ, anoints and seals us in His Spirit who is our guarantee (1:21-22). "The numerous promises of God, given through the mouths of many prophets at different times and places, all converge like so many lines at one point, the Son of God whom Paul and his companions now proclaim. There is no ambiguity, *Yes* and *No*, about the Son of God. It is as if God is saying, 'Jesus Christ, my Son, is my 'yes' to every promise I have ever made. He fulfills everything I have ever said.' From God's side, as well as from ours, everything is focused on Christ…"[23] Our response is to say "Amen!" to the glory of God. Amen is saying "So be it. It is True! I agree." It is belief with an exclamation point at the end. In the disappointment and *no's* you are experiencing, will you say "Amen!" that Jesus Christ is the YES to all God's promises to you?

## What are You Fighting For?
## II Corinthians 1:23-2:4

Even as "the Corinthians' criticisms heaped internal grief upon his external miseries,"[24] Paul stays focused on the goal of the Corinthians' joy in the faith. Out of his "wounded love" Paul responds with transparency

---

22 Murray J. Harris, *The Second Epistle to the Corinthians* (Eerdmans Publishing Co: Grand Rapids, MI, 2005), 195.

23 Paul Barnett, *The Message of 2 Corinthians* (Inter-Varsity Press: Downers Grove, IL, 1988), 39.

24 R. Kent Hughes, *2 Corinthians: Power in Weakness* (Crossway Books: Wheaton, IL, 2006), 44.

and overflowing love to the Corinthians. As John Piper says, "What's at stake in the fight for joy is the radiance of the worth of Jesus made visible for the world to see in the sacrifices of love flowing from the joy of blood-bought, soul-satisfied, Christ-exalting people. When Paul says to the Corinthians, 'We work with you for your joy' (2 Cor 1:24), he was not saying, 'We pamper you.' He was saying, 'We prepare you for radical, Christ-exalting sacrifices of love.'"[25] How will you respond when wounded? Will you stay open, even in the raw pain, like Paul? Or will you shut down or lash out? Bitter unbelief or a seemingly foolish faith filled with wounds and scars? Which will lead you to joy and to Jesus and God's glory?

## Where Forgiveness Leads
## II Corinthians 2:5-11

Paul then asks the church to take another radical step: forgiveness and restoration of a man they had disciplined. Who was this now-repentant man and what had he done? One of Paul's mercies is he does not list his name. Most current commentators believe he was a Corinthian who had openly opposed Paul and his teaching and had probably suffered excommunication. "For Paul, forgiveness was of paramount importance for the sinner and for the church."[26] Paul sees forgiveness as a matter of obedience (2:9). "Obedience to God's Word demands doing the hard work of church discipline, and then the hard work of forgiving."[27] The same Greek root for *grace* is found in *forgive*, to intentionally grace the one who does not deserve it, to give freely. Satan's tactic would be to harden resolve against the offender and divide the church, the body of Christ. Jesus' goal is found in his prayer (Luke 11:4) to forgive as we have been forgiven. Paul shows the goal of church discipline is "the glory of Christ, the purity of the church, and the restoration of the sinner."[28] Paul, wounded and offended, leads the Corinthians to show love and forgiveness, to defeat Satan, and to point to Christ, the Son of God and YES and Amen to all God's promises.

---

25 John Piper, *When I Don't Desire God: How to Fight for Joy* (Crossways Books: Wheaton, IL, 2004), 140.

26 Hughes, 50.

27 Hughes, 50.

28 *Spirit of the Reformation Study Bible* (Zondervan: Grand Rapids, MI, 2003), 1874, Notes.

# Week 4: The Reality of Inability
## II Corinthians 2:14-3:18

*Questions marked with an \* are for those doing Bible Study Express.*

## Day 1: The Real Aroma of Christ

**Read II Corinthians 2:14-17.** Read also Colossians 2:13-15. As you read about God leading us in triumphal procession in Christ (which is a reference to a conquering Roman army's victory parade), do you think Paul means we are like the victorious soldiers or like the prisoners on display? Why?

Get in touch with your senses. Describe what you think the aroma of Christ "smells" like.*

What does it mean that Christ in us is like the "smell of death" to some and "the fragrance of life" to others?

Rewrite II Corinthians 2:14-16 in your own words.*

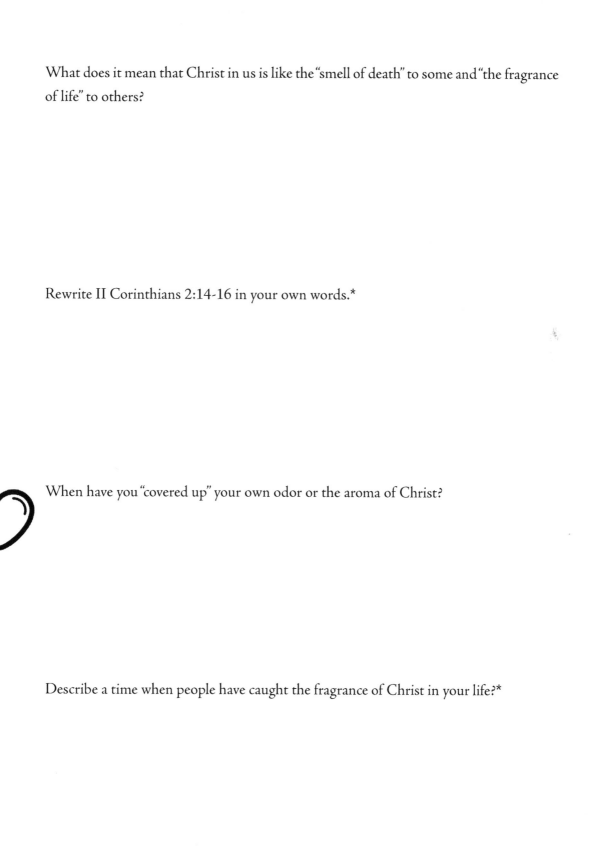

When have you "covered up" your own odor or the aroma of Christ?

Describe a time when people have caught the fragrance of Christ in your life?*

From your description of the aroma of Christ, which of His qualities do you most desire to radiate to those around you?* Ask Christ boldly to transform you in this area.

Consolidate the message of II Corinthians 2:14-3:18 into one sentence. Share that sentence with a family member, friend, or someone in your group this week.

*Optional: Do discovery sheet on II Corinthians 2:14-3:18 found at end of the weekly lesson.*

# Day 2: Real References

**Read II Corinthians 2:14-3:18.** Religious leaders of the time often came to a new city with letters of reference. What does Paul say is his reference letter?*

How does Paul's ministry style differ from religious leaders he described?

If your spouse, children, or close friends were to read what you've written on their hearts, what would they say?

Who has "written on your heart" like Paul wrote on the Corinthians' hearts?*

What about that person has most deeply affected you or changed you?*

 It has been said that you may be the only letter from Christ that some people will read. What would they read and what would you want them to read?

Ask your group to pray for you that you may be a Christ influence on those around you. Be specific about how you most want to affect people for Christ.

**Read II Corinthians 2:14-3:18.** What is the task that Paul refers to in vs. 2:16 and what is his answer in vs. 3:4-6 to his question of *"who is equal to such a task?"*

From what you know about Paul, was he competent? How do you think he dealt with his competence and the task before him?

What does Paul mean that his confidence and competence were from God?*

Give an example where you have either killed or been killed by the "letter."

Give an example where you have given or received life by the "Spirit."

 Do you tend to be responsible and follow through and get things done right? (Do it right or die trying.) Or do you stumble through life, a little surprised when things actually do go right? (Your theme song is "*Que sera, sera.*")

When you read vs. 4-6, do you feel confused or relieved?*

 Think of a task or project you are currently involved with and how you might do it differently, with a competence that comes from God. How could you give life and be a "new-covenant" minister in this project and in your home or work environment.*

## Day 4: The Reality of the Old Covenant

 **Read II Corinthians 3:1-18.** Read Exodus 34:27-35. What is the basis of the old covenant?*

Why was Moses' face glowing and why was it fading? Why did Moses wear a veil?*

From II Corinthians 3:7-18, compare and contrast the old and new covenant

OLD COVENANT                                             NEW COVENANT

What does *glory* mean in this passage?

What kind of veils do you hide behind? What masks do you put on to keep people from seeing the "real" you?*

What scares you the most about people seeing the real you?*

 Ask God to give you courage to see how you veil yourself and how to remove the veil. Ask your group to pray for you to remove one veil this week (and be accountable to them!).*

# Day 5: The Reality of the New Covenant

 **Read II Corinthians 3:1-18.** Read also Jeremiah 31:31-34 and Romans 3:19-24. Through Jesus Christ we have gone through a total "paradigm shift" from a performance and law-based paradigm to a believing and grace-based paradigm. What are similarities and differences between the old and new covenant?*

What is the basis for Paul's bold hope in II Corinthians 3:12?

What are the some of the results of living in the new covenant you see in this passage?*

Do you think of turning to the Lord as a one-time event or an ongoing process? Why?

Paul uses confidence (vs. 4), boldness (vs. 12), and freedom (vs. 17) to describe a new covenant lifestyle. What is the basis of Paul's confidence, boldness, and freedom?

Do those words describe your lifestyle and the way you communicate Christ to others?

Do you think that Christians can still live in the old covenant paradigm?

Based on the new covenant in Christ, what is the Christian's relationship to the law?*

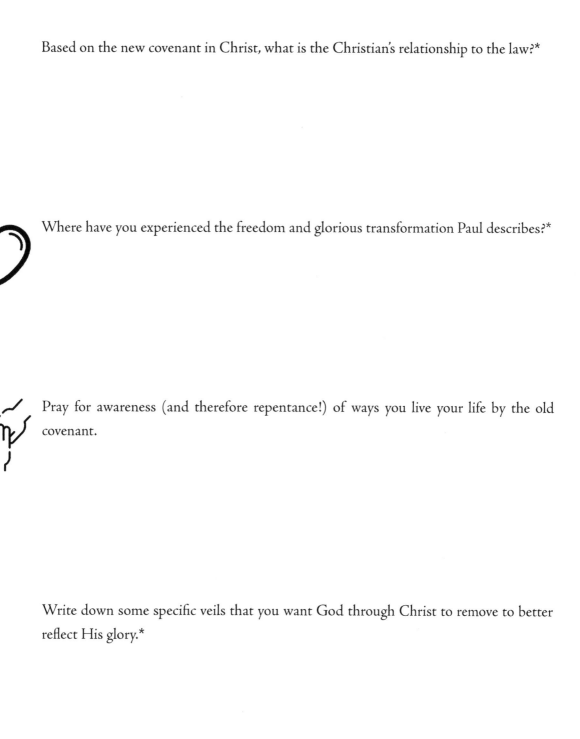

Where have you experienced the freedom and glorious transformation Paul describes?*

Pray for awareness (and therefore repentance!) of ways you live your life by the old covenant.

Write down some specific veils that you want God through Christ to remove to better reflect His glory.*

# OPTIONAL PERSONAL DISCOVERY SHEET

II Corinthians 2:14-3:18

## CONTENT

List the main points from this Scripture.

## DIVISIONS

Divide content into 2-4 main sections and write a sentence for each division.

## ESSENCE OF PASSAGE

Write a short sentence (10 words or less!) that gives the thrust of the passage.

## ESSENTIAL QUESTION/AIM

Write the main "transformational truth" to remember from studying this Scripture. Make this as short and simple as possible. It helps to put it in the form of a question to link it to application.

## APPLICATIONS

Write specific questions or challenges to help put the aim into action or answer the question. Are there specific areas in which you need to repent? To believe God and his Word? To live out and apply the gospel?

# Week 4: The Reality of Inability
## II Corinthians 2:14-3:18

## GROUP DISCUSSION

✓ *How have you experienced the new covenant lifestyle Paul describes in these verses?*

## TEACHING TIME

### Warning! Detour Ahead

Paul's Six-Chapter Detour

Landmarks So You Don't Get Lost

The Scent of a Christian

### The Paradoxes of the Christian Life

Triumph through Defeat

Confident Submission, not Self-Made Success

Life through Death

Strength in Weakness

Beholding is Becoming

## Drop the Veil!  The New Covenant vs. Old Covenant

Inner Confidence vs. Outer Competence

Freedom and Boldness vs. Fading and Failing

What does new covenant Christianity look and smell like?

## REALITY CHECK

*Where are you still living in the old covenant? Where do you need to drop a veil? How will your scent attract people to Christ this week?*

## REAL REALITY: SCRIPTURE MEDITATION

*BELIEVE IT.  IT'S TRUE, AND TRUE FOR YOU. AMEN!*

*But when one turns to the Lord, the veil is removed. Now the Lord is the Spirit, and where the Spirit of the Lord is, there is freedom. And we all, with unveiled face, beholding the glory of the Lord, are being transformed into the same image from one degree of glory to another. For this comes from the Lord who is the Spirit. II Corinthians 3:16-18*

# Reality Christianity:
# Radiating Christ in Our Cracked Lives
## Week 4: II Corinthians 2:14-3:18
*The Reality of Inability / The Reality of our Covenantal God*

## Paul's Detour:  Defending His Real Ministry
## II Corinthians 2:14-7:4

In II Corinthians, Paul defends his calling as an apostle, his ministry, and his actions to the people he had helped lead to the Lord Jesus Christ. In the first two chapters, Paul gives his credentials and defends his travel plans. He takes a six-chapter detour (2:14-7:4) to explain what new-covenant Christianity looks, smells, and "feels" like in contrast to those who are trying to influence the Corinthians to live "old-covenant" self-generated, law-focused lives. In these chapters, Paul shows by his own life, the Corinthians' lives, and most importantly, Jesus Christ, that Christianity is all about Jesus Christ radiating his fragrance (2:15) and light (4:6) through our cracked lives (4:7). It is not about success, but about submission (2:14). It is about being compelled by his love (5:14), being ambassadors of reconciliation (6:20), and hoping for holiness (7:1).

**What's our "job" in all this?** Believing and beholding the glory of the Lord (3:18) and being transformed— not by our competence—but by the sufficiency and competency of Christ (3:4-6).

In 7:5 Paul picks back up with his trip from Troas to Macedonia as he speaks to repentant believers to complete their commitment to give. The tone of the letter changes to a sober warning in chapters 10-13 as Paul speaks to the unrepentant.

## Radiating Christ:  The Scent of Jesus
## II Corinthians 2:14-17

Most commentators agree that the triumphal procession (2:14) refers to "lavish victory parades celebrated in Rome after great battles. God is depicted as the sovereign victor, with Christ as the general, leading the victory procession, and Paul as 'captured' by Christ but now joyfully following him. . . The picture here reflects a recurring theme throughout 2 Corinthians, namely, the contrast between the believer's apparent (temporal) defeat and the believer's actual (spiritual) victory."[29]

---

29 [1] *ESV Study Bible*, Notes on II Corinthians 2:14.

**Welcome to the paradox of the Christian life.** Triumph through defeat. Life through death. Strength in weakness. Here Paul is showing that "his suffering, being led to death in the Roman procession, is the medium through which God is revealing himself."[30] It is the opposite message the super apostles are preaching to the Corinthians.

Scent is a powerful emotional evoker and memory machine. Aren't there certain smells that bring you right back to your grandmother's kitchen, your dad's car, your high school lunchroom? Here, the fragrance the world responds to is Christ's sacrifice (he was crushed for our sins, Isa. 53:5) on the cross. Our lives too will smell of the "crushed fragrance of suffering and daily death . . . the gospel emanating from our weakness and death. . .The fragrance of Christ can only come through being led in triumphal procession as captives of the cross."[31] No wonder it is life to some and death to others. Are you a captive of the cross? What scent do you radiate to the world? Or do you try to hide or neutralize your smell?

## New Covenant:  Inner Confidence, Not Outer Competence
## II Corinthians 3:1-6

Paul contrasts his credentials (the inner fruit of changed lives) with the competing false teachers written reference letters. The church is his living letter of recommendation. The Corinthians were tattooed on his heart, "the Greek perfect tense indicating that they were permanently engraved there."[32] How have you invested in people's lives so they are engraved on your heart? Paul writes that his ministry is in the sight of God (2:17) in contrast to his competitors' peddling God's word. "To walk in the sight of God requires total honesty with him and ourselves. . . .it means there are no areas of denial. . .A man who walks in the sight of God is more interested in his inner reality than his outer reputation."[33]

**Who is sufficient for these things?** (2:16) "The work of the gospel (and the Christian life as a whole) can never be carried out based on human ability or by human means. As Paul goes on to explain, our 'sufficiency' comes only from God by means of his grace ('sufficient' translates the Greek *hikanos*, 'sufficient, competent, qualified.'"[34] Another paradox: Paul's confidence "was rooted in his inadequacy."[35] R. Kent Hughes, a faithful preacher and commentator, has this quote by Oswald Chambers framed by his desk: "God can achieve his purpose either through the absence of human power and resources, or the abandonment of reliance on them. All through history God has chosen and used nobodies, because their unusual dependence on him made possible the unique display of his power and grace. He chose

---

30  R. Kent Hughes, *2 Corinthians: Power in Weakness* (Crossway Books: Wheaton, IL, 2006), 56.

31  Hughes, 57.

32  Paul Barnett, *The Message of 2 Corinthians* (Inter-Varsity Press: Downers Grove, IL, 1988), 61.

33  Ray C. Stedman, *Authentic Christianity* (Discovery House Publishers: Grand Rapids, MI, 1996), 38

34  *ESV Study Bible*, Notes on II Corinthians 3:5.

35  Hughes, 68.

and used somebodies only when they renounced dependence on their natural abilities and resources."[36] How are you depending on God's power and grace? The paradox continues as Paul contrasts the old and new covenant. The old is symbolized by Moses (see Ex. 32-34) giving the law which brought death and condemnation because of the Israelite's inability to obey it all. Even then, it was glorious. The new covenant (Jer. 31:31-34) is fulfilled in Jesus Christ and lived out in the Spirit in confidence, freedom, and inside-out transformation.

## New Covenant: Freedom and Boldness, Not Fading and Failing
## II Corinthians 3:7-18

These verses give us a taste of the real Christian life. Many Christians still live in the old-covenant paradigm because they are so scared to drop their veils. "The satanic lie is that in order to be liked or accepted we must appear capable or successful. Therefore, we either project capability (the extrovert) or we seek to hide our failure (the introvert). The new covenant offers the opposite. If we will admit our inadequacy, we can have God's adequacy, and all we have sought vainly to produce (confidence, success, impact, integrity, and reality) is given to us at the point of our inability. The key is to take away the veil."[37]

We could meditate on 3:18 for the rest of this study and not plumb its depths. What does it mean to behold the glory of the Lord? "The word translated 'beholding' (Greek *katoptrizō*) can mean 'behold' or 'reflect' or 'look at in a mirror,' and commentators support all three views. In this context, however, the connection with a mirror does not seem to be necessary to the word, and the meaning 'behold' seems more consistent with the idea of having the veil removed and therefore being able to see God's glory, in contrast to the unbelieving Jews who still have a veil blocking their vision. As a result of beholding the Lord through the ministry of the Spirit, the believer is being transformed (a process of sanctification over time, not an instantaneous change) into the same image of God that was distorted at the fall. The 'image' of God includes every way in which humans are like God, such as their moral character, their true knowledge, their many God-given abilities, and their dominion over creation, to be exercised with dependence on God as the Creator and giver of all things."[38] May we all with unveiled faces behold the glory of the Lord and be transformed!

---

36 Hughes, 69.

37 Stedman 94.

38 *ESV Study Bible*, Notes on II Corinthians 3:18.

# Week 5: The Reality of Cracked Pots
## II Corinthians 4:1-5:10

*Questions marked with an * are for those doing Bible Study Express.*

## Day 1: The Real Thing:  Jesus Christ

 **Read II Corinthians 4:1-5:10.** Read Hebrews 1:1-3 and Colossians 1:15-20. From these passages, relish and describe Jesus.*

What is the *gospel* Paul refers to in 4:3-4?*

How would you communicate what the gospel is to someone unfamiliar with Christianity?

From this passage, why does Paul say some people do not believe?*

How can you avoid having the gospel veiled in your own life?

What is Paul's ministry that he refers to in 4:1?*

How does Paul conduct his ministry?

Paul speaks of not losing heart in II Cor. 4:1, 16. What causes you to lose heart?*  What helps you find courage?*

*Turn your eyes upon Jesus. Look full in his wonderful face and the things of earth will grow strangely dim in the light of His glory and grace.* (Hymn refrain by Helen Lemmel)
Meditate on the glory of God in the face of Christ. How do you turn your eyes upon Jesus? Write down specific ways every day where you can turn your eyes more and more upon Jesus.*

Give specific ways that the truths found in this passage will affect how you pray for, relate to, and reach out to people outside the faith.

Consolidate the message of II Corinthians 4:1-5:10 into one sentence. Share that sentence with a family member, friend, or someone in your group this week.

*Optional: Do discovery sheet on II Corinthians 4:1-5:10 found at end of the weekly lesson.*

**Read II Corinthians 4:7-5:10.** What is the treasure which Paul speaks of?*

What visual images throughout this passage does Paul use to describe the reality of this temporal life or the vessel that holds the treasure?

List the four things Paul says he is and is not in vs. 4:8-9:*

|  | IS | BUT | NOT |
|---|---|---|---|
| 1. |  |  |  |
| 2. |  |  |  |
| 3. |  |  |  |
| 4. |  |  |  |

Which emotion or circumstance from the left-hand column do you most identify with?*
What has been your response to that emotion or situation?

Look again at the two columns. Why was Paul able to have "right-column" responses to his "left-column" circumstances and emotions?

What does Paul mean when he talks about carrying the death and revealing the life of Jesus in his body?

What kind of "pot" or container are you?* Think in terms of dinnerware. Are you:

_____fragile, special-occasion china

_____an on-display but never-used heirloom

_____disposable dishes and paper plates

_____everyday, overused, and chipped plates

_____other. Describe:

What kind of container do you want to be?

Are you willing to be (and look like a) cracked pot, if God shines through all the broken areas?

List ways that God's all-surpassing power can be better revealed to others in your life this week.

Share with your group one "crack" in your life where God has revealed His power or Christ has radiated through you.*

**Read II Corinthians 4:13-18.** Read also Hebrews 11:1-12:3. In II Corinthians 4:13, Paul speaks of believing and then speaking. What does Paul believe?

What is the benefit that Paul speaks of in vs. 15?*

In II Corinthians 4:16-18, Paul is dealing with the double reality of present life and the `promised life to come. What are the hard realities?

What are the holy realities?

Where do you feel like you are "wasting away?"

Write down and share with your group where you have experienced inner renewal.*

Give practical ways we can fix our eyes on the unseen, eternal realities in this seen, temporal world.*

**Read II Corinthians 5:1-10.** Read also I Corinthians 15:42-58, Philippians 3:21 and Revelation 21:4. How does Paul contrast his current earthly body to his heavenly life and body to come?*

What *guarantee* do we have of what's to come? What helps you believe beyond this life?

How do the verses you read today give you hope?*

As you read this specific passage and "think biblically," for what purpose has God created you?

You may have heard the statement "so heavenly-minded, they're no earthly good." Would you agree or disagree with that statement and why?*

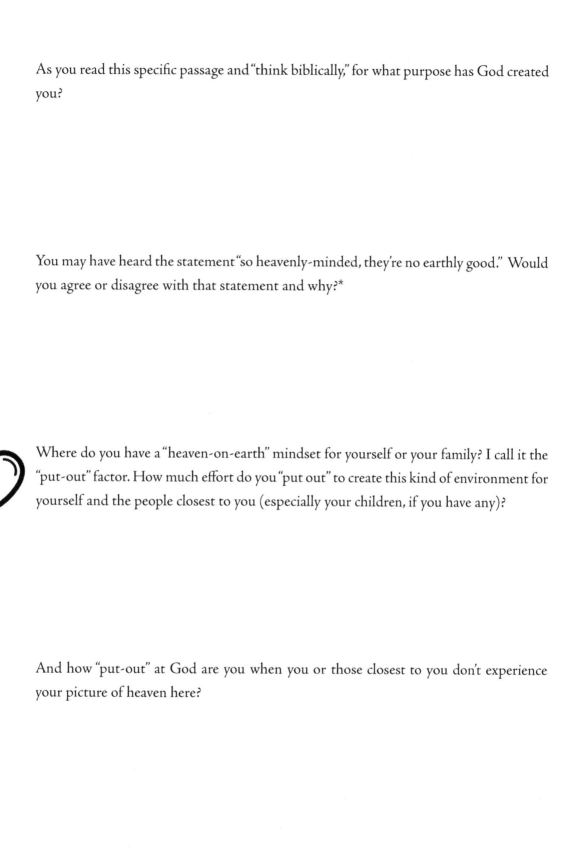 Where do you have a "heaven-on-earth" mindset for yourself or your family? I call it the "put-out" factor. How much effort do you "put out" to create this kind of environment for yourself and the people closest to you (especially your children, if you have any)?

And how "put-out" at God are you when you or those closest to you don't experience your picture of heaven here?

Do you think of comfort on this earth as a "right?"

 Do you enjoy or fear thinking about heaven?

Where do you groan or long for heaven?*

# Day 5: Real Motivation

**Read II Corinthians 5:1-10.** Read also Ephesians 2:8-9, I Corinthians 3:10-15 and I Peter 1:13-25. List two or three elements of your Christian faith that are central to you even though you cannot see them.

Why are they important to you?

What motivates Paul to persevere in his ministry on earth?* What is his goal?* What is your goal?*

What is the judgment seat of Christ? Who and what will Jesus Christ judge?

 What does it mean to you personally to walk by faith and not by sight?* Give an example.

*Therefore judge nothing before the appointed time; wait till the Lord comes. He will bring to light what is hidden in the darkness and will expose the motives of men's hearts. At that time each will receive his praise from God. I Cor. 4:5.* Pray that the Lord will reveal the motives of your heart and both repent and rejoice over what He reveals. Remember how He views you and is pleased with you in Christ.

As you meditate on appearing before Jesus Christ, evaluate your heart motivations and activities. What will last and what will burn?

How does this drive you back to Christ for encouragement and hope for transformation?*

Ask your group for specific prayer on how to love and please the Lord more.*

# OPTIONAL PERSONAL DISCOVERY SHEET

II Corinthians 4:1-5:10

## CONTENT

List the main points from this Scripture.

## DIVISIONS

Divide content into 2-4 main sections and write a sentence for each division.

## ESSENCE OF PASSAGE

Write a short sentence (10 words or less!) that gives the thrust of the passage.

## ESSENTIAL QUESTION/AIM

Write the main "transformational truth" to remember from studying this Scripture. Make this as short and simple as possible. It helps to put it in the form of a question to link it to application.

## APPLICATIONS

Write specific questions or challenges to help put the aim into action or answer the question. Are there specific areas in which you need to repent? To believe God and his Word? To live out and apply the gospel?

# Week 5: The Reality of Cracked Pots
## II Corinthians 4:1-5:10

## GROUP DISCUSSION

✓ *Paul uses the example of our bodies and homes to refocus us from the temporal to the eternal. In this last week, how much of your thoughts, energies, desires, and disappointments were focused on your physical body or home?*

## TEACHING TIME

### RELISH THE RADIATING CHRIST

**He radiates through your cracks.**
**II Corinthians 4:1-12**

Hard Reality:

Holy Reality:

### RELISH THE RENEWING CHRIST

**He renews you daily.**
**II Corinthians 4:13-18**

Hard Reality:

Holy Reality:

## RELISH THE RESURRECTING CHRIST

### He reveals your true longings and goals.
### II Corinthians 5:1-10

Hard Reality:


Holy Reality:


## REALITY CHECK

*Do you treasure the Treasure or are you consumed by the container? Where can you begin to trust God to relish and reveal Christ more than focusing on the packaging?*

## REAL REALITY: SCRIPTURE MEDITATION

*BELIEVE IT. IT'S TRUE, AND TRUE FOR YOU. AMEN!*

*Therefore, we do not lose heart. Though outwardly we are wasting away, yet inwardly we are being renewed day by day. For our light and momentary troubles are achieving for us an eternal glory that far outweighs them all. So we fix our eyes not on what is seen, but on what is unseen. For what is seen is temporary, but what is unseen is eternal. II Corinthians 4:16-18*

# Reality Christianity:
# Radiating Christ in Our Cracked Lives
## Week 5: II Corinthians 4:1-5:10
*The Reality of Cracked Pots: The Reality of our Radiating God*

## Paul's Message: Don't Lose Heart. Live the Paradox.
## II Corinthians 4:1-5:10

Paul's repeated theme in these very "real" verses: **Do not lose heart** (4:1, 16; 5:6, 8) in the midst of criticism, hard hearts and blind eyes, afflictions and persecutions, decaying bodies, futility, and longings for heaven. II Corinthians is about living the paradox: seeing light in darkness, living like Christ in his death and resurrection, radiating Christ's light in cracked pots, experiencing outer decay and inner renewal, longing for our heavenly home as we aim to please the Lord and walk by faith. Paul knows one of our biggest battles was to believe in the midst of this perplexing world, to be of good courage (5:6, 8) when we fear, to not lose heart (4:1, 16) when our hearts are breaking. He gives a roadmap to treasure the true Treasure instead of being consumed by our cracked containers (4:6-7); to keep our eyes fixed on the eternal instead of the temporary (4:17-18); to walk by faith (5:7) as we long to see the face of Jesus Christ (4:6) and be truly home.

## DO NOT LOSE HEART! Relish Jesus Christ as Lord and Light
## II Corinthians 4:1-6

God mercifully gave Paul a ministry, this man who hated Christ, persecuted His people, and worked the old-covenant Mosaic law as his means of advancement. God converted and commissioned Paul as an apostle to the Gentiles and showed him how much he must suffer for the sake of Jesus' name (Acts 9:16). This new-covenant ministry, which he wrote of in II Corinthians 3 of "everything coming from God, nothing from me"[39] resulting in unveiled glory, freedom, and transformation is a paradox and mystery. Paul's purpose is testifying to the gospel of God's grace (Acts 20:24). He preaches Jesus Christ as Lord (4:5). That's the gospel in four words: *Jesus Christ is Lord*.

**Jesus** means the 'Lord saves,' is "the name given to the Son of God at his incarnation and signifies that the Lord's salvation came when Jesus was born."[40]

---

39  Ray C. Stedman, *Authentic Christianity* (Discovery House Publishers: Grand Rapids, MI, 1996), 137.

40  R. Kent Hughes, *2 Corinthians: Power in Weakness* (Crossway Books: Wheaton, IL, 2006), 86.

**Christ** means 'anointed one or Messiah' and "speaks of his being the fulfillment of Old Testament prophecy"[41] (I Cor. 15:3-4).

**Lord** "declares the fact that the crucified Christ has been exalted by God through the resurrection to the position of lordship in Heaven and that he is ruler of the world . . . 'so that at the name of Jesus every knee should bow, in heaven and on earth and under the earth, and every tongue confess that Jesus Christ is Lord, to the glory of God the Father.' (Phil. 2:10-11) . . . When you confess that 'Jesus Christ is Lord' you at once confess his *incarnation* and his *Messiahship* and his *lordship*, sealed by his glorious resurrection as he now forever reigns."[42]

John Piper writes, "The gospel is news about the death and resurrection of Jesus (I Cor. 15:1-4). It is a word to be heard. And in this hearing, there is something to be seen: 'The light . . . of the glory of Christ.' In the hearing is the seeing. The Lord opens the eyes of the heart to see the glory of Christ in the Word. God has chosen in this age to reveal himself to the world mainly through the incarnate Word, Jesus Christ, by means of the written Word, the Bible."[43]

## DO NOT LOSE HEART! Glory in the God Who Resurrects and Renews Us
## II Corinthians 4:7-18

We do not lose heart because our Creator God has shone light into our darkness and removed our veils so that we can sing the hymn, *"Turn your eyes upon Jesus and look full in his wonderful face and the things of earth will grow strangely dim in the light of his glory and grace."*

Paul states we have the Treasure (the light of the knowledge of the glory of God in the face of Jesus Christ) in clay jars, the everyday common containers of the Mideast. Today's equivalent would be our fast-food packaging. We radiate the light of Jesus Christ through the cracks and creases of our common, everyday lives; we show God's power through our weakness. "This is Christian realism. Christians are never powerful in themselves but are only vessels in which God's power is exhibited. . .Paul is graphically and categorically stating that our weakness is essential to and necessary for the display of his power. . .We do not become powerful. We remain weak. We do not grow in power. We grow in weakness. We go from weakness to weakness, which is to remain vessels of his power—ever weak and ever strong."[44]

In 4:8-9, Paul reveals the reality of his ministry: afflicted, perplexed, persecuted, struck down. The contrast is significant. Paul was not crushed. Jesus was (Isa. 53:5). Paul was not driven to despair or

---

41 Hughes, 86.

42 Hughes, 86.

43 John Piper, *When I Don't Desire God: How to Fight for Joy* (Crossways Books: Wheaton, IL, 2004), 140.

44 Hughes, 90.

forsaken. Jesus was (Mk. 15:34). Paul was not destroyed. Jesus was crucified (Lk. 23:33), dead and buried. But we do not lose heart because we know that God who raised the Lord Jesus from the dead will raise us also with Jesus together into his presence (4:14). This life is not futile, and we are not fools (I Cor 15). The Resurrection is reality.

We also do not lose heart because of the awesome paradoxical truths of inner daily renewal in the midst of our outer decaying bodies and the incomparable weight of glory as compared to our 'light momentary afflictions' (4:16-18). Paul says we can train ourselves to have an eternal perspective. "Paul's argument here is very simple. The visible things of this life are but transient manifestations of abiding realities that cannot now be seen. . . The truly important thing in life is not to adjust oneself to the changing form, but to relate always to the abiding truth."[45] We see our destiny with the eyes of faith (Hebrews 11).

## DO NOT LOSE HEART! Walk by Faith as We Wait to Go Home
## II Corinthians 4:1-5:10

Paul, the tentmaker, uses a tent as an example of this temporary life in comparison to our permanent heavenly home. Paul expresses his longing for his true home. Dr. Lyle Dorsett stated for *Christianity Today* what turned him from agnosticism to faith. "When G. K. Chesterton said that after he became a Christian, he finally knew why he always felt he had been **homesick at home**, the light went on. I recognized that this 'longing' for home had driven me to continually seek a more comfortable place to live and companions who could bring me happiness and fulfillment. . . I had begun to assume that I would never find contentment and therefore must settle for a degree of inner desperation. Chesterton, and eventually C. S. Lewis, who admirably addressed the same theme ('If I find in myself a desire which no experience in this world can satisfy, the most probable explanation is that I was made for another world.') helped me see that heaven is my home, and Jesus Christ has prepared a place for me there."[46]

Paul walks by faith as he waits. "Faith is the human response to a divine offer."[47] Paul aims to please the Lord as he considers the judgment seat of Christ (5:10) "The teaching about the judgment seat before which all must come, believers included, reminds us that we have been saved, not for a life of aimlessness or indifference, but for a life of serving the Lord. The balanced view . . . is that while we are justified by faith alone, the faith that justifies is expressed by love and obedience."[48]

---

45 Stedman, 140.

46 Lyle Dorsett. *Christianity Today* http://www.christianitytoday.com/ct/2008/novemberweb-only/147-11.0.html Oct 12, 2009.

47 Stedman, 154.

48 Paul Barnett, *The Message of 2 Corinthians* (Inter-Varsity Press: Downers Grove, IL, 1988), 104.

# Week 6: The Reality of Brokenness
## II Corinthians 5:11-6:13

*Questions marked with an * are for those doing Bible Study Express.*

## Day 1: Real Motivation

**Read II Corinthians 5:11-6:13.** False teachers were influencing the Corinthian church and attacking Paul. What accusations might Paul's opponents have made about him and what was Paul's response?

How was Paul's ministry different from these false teachers or "super-apostles" as he called them in II Corinthians 11:5?

What does it mean *to fear the Lord* (vs. 5:9-11)?*

In vs. 5:14, what does *for Christ's love compels us* mean? Does it mean Christ's love for us, our love for Christ, or Christ's love flowing through us to others? Give a reason (and Bible verse) for your answer.

What motivates Paul?*

How can a Christian be motivated by both the fear of the Lord (vs. 5:11) and the love of Christ (vs. 5:14)?*

II Corinthians 5:12 is a key "get real" verse. Where do you take pride in what's seen rather than what's in the heart?* Is it in your physical appearance, clothing and accessories, home, car, your performance at work or church, your children's behavior, your relationship with your spouse?

How does it make you feel when that "veil" fails or is ripped away?

Meditate on the love of Christ for you.*

Do you know how much you are loved by Christ? Did you once know and have forgotten? If it is not fresh and you're not filled with gratitude, don't wallow or whip yourself up. Simply repent and ask God to give you a renewed sense of Christ's love for you.

What compels you? Spend a few minutes examining what you do and why you do it

Where do you live for yourself? Where do you live for Christ?

How could you live for Christ more this week?*

Consolidate the message of II Corinthians 5:11-6:3 into one sentence. Share that sentence with a family member, friend, or someone in your group this week.

*Optional: Do discovery sheet on II Corinthians 5:11-6:3 found at end of the weekly lesson.*

# Day 2: The Message of Reconciliation

 **Read II Corinthians 5:11-6:2.** In II Corinthians 5:18-20, Paul uses reconciled or reconciliation five times. What is reconciliation?*

What does it mean to be reconciled to God?*

What has Christ done to make reconciliation possible?*

What does it mean to be a new creation in Christ?* (See also John 3:3-8, 16-18; Rom. 12:2; Eph 4:22-24; and Col. 3:1-11.) Is it a one-time event, a process, or both? Why do you say so?

 What has meant the most to you about your new relationship with God through Christ (even if you can't remember a time as an "old" creation)?*

 Do a reality check. Have you experienced what it is like to be a new creation in Christ?* If you don't know, simply make sure by telling God you don't know, acknowledging your sin, acknowledging that only Christ can reconcile you to God and make you righteous before God, releasing yourself to God, and asking Him to make you a new creation in Christ. It's done. If you know that you are a new creation, thank God and pray to live like a new creation in one specific area of your life this week.

**Read II Corinthians 5:11-6:2.** Paul was speaking to Christians at Corinth. Why would he urge Christians to be reconciled to God?

What does it mean that we have the ministry of reconciliation?* That we are Christ's ambassadors?*

Think of both your horizontal (with other people) and vertical (with God) relationships. What does it feel like to have unresolved conflict or a broken relationship?*

Do you have a fight, flight, or freeze response to conflict?

 Where do you need to reconcile broken relationships?* (With yourself, others, God?) Make a short "reconciliation" list.

Knowing your natural tendency on dealing with conflict and knowing that God gives the courage and ability to "re-enter" broken relationships, pray for wisdom, courage, and love to be Christ's ambassador and enter the ministry of reconciliation.

**Read II Corinthians 5:17-21.** The heart of the gospel is in these verses. Take time to think and write what these terms mean:

New creation:

Old vs. new:

Reconciled/ reconciliation:

Sins:

Sin:

Righteousness of God:

In Him, in Christ:

Reword as simply as possible II Corinthians 5:17-21 so that you could share it with someone unfamiliar with Christianity.*

What motivates you to share the gospel? What stops you from sharing the gospel?

 How can you grow in your awe and love of God the Father and our Lord Jesus Christ this week?*

List ways you have been forgiven and reconciled to God. Thank Him.

 Share with your family, friends or small group a brief testimony of how you have been reconciled to God or been made new in Christ, and use your words to state the truth of II Corinthians 5:17-21.* Begin developing an intentional, authentic relationship with someone with the purpose of being a loving ambassador for Christ.*

**Read II Corinthians 6:3-13.** List Paul's hardships.

Which can you most relate to?* And which do you most fear experiencing?*

Paul's "hard" realities are also laced with "holy" realities. List virtues Paul exhibits in the midst of his hardships.

Which of those virtues fly out the window first if you are hungry, exhausted, under attack, or in pain?

Which of those holy realities do you most need or desire?

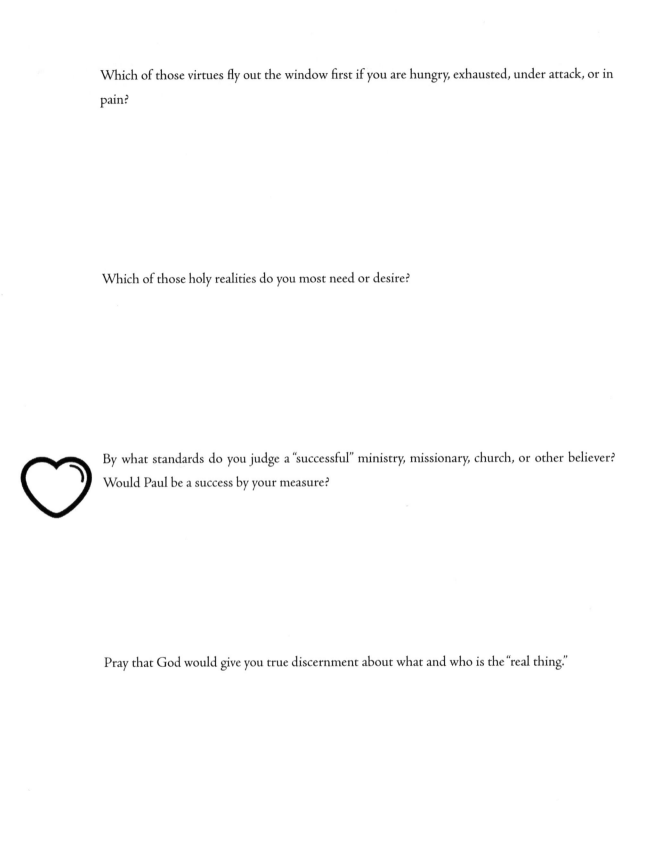

By what standards do you judge a "successful" ministry, missionary, church, or other believer? Would Paul be a success by your measure?

Pray that God would give you true discernment about what and who is the "real thing."

Paul pleads with the Corinthians to open wide their hearts to him as he has opened his heart to them. Are you willing to continue to be vulnerable and open with people who do not reciprocate or may even criticize you (and yes, that does include your children)?

 Stop and spend time relishing our reconciling God and your "forever" reconciled relationship to Him through Jesus Christ.

Encourage someone who has been in the thick of the hard and holy reality of ministry. List someone you will encourage and someone you will open your heart to this week.

# OPTIONAL PERSONAL DISCOVERY SHEET

II Corinthians 5:11-6:13

## CONTENT

List the main points from this Scripture.

## DIVISIONS

Divide content into 2-4 main sections and write a sentence for each division.

## ESSENCE OF PASSAGE

Write a short sentence (10 words or less!) that gives the thrust of the passage.

## ESSENTIAL QUESTION/AIM

Write the main "transformational truth" to remember from studying this Scripture. Make this as short and simple as possible. It helps to put it in the form of a question to link it to application.

## APPLICATIONS

Write specific questions or challenges to help put the aim into action or answer the question. Are there specific areas in which you need to repent? To believe God and his Word? To live out and apply the gospel?

# Week 6: The Reality of Brokenness and the Reality of Our Reconciling God
## II Corinthians 5:9-6:13

## GROUP DISCUSSION

✓ *How can you be motivated by both the fear of the Lord and the love of Christ?*

## TEACHING TIME

### WHAT'S YOUR MOTIVATION?
### II Corinthians 5:9-15

*The Mystery of the Double Reality: Reverent Awe and Love*

### WHAT'S YOUR MINISTRY?
### II Corinthians 5:16-6:2

*The Miracle of Reconciliation: Restoration of Relationship*

### WHAT'S YOUR METHOD?
### II Corinthians 6:3-13

*The Courage to Be Real: Live a Life of Risk and Openness*

## REALITY CHECK

*Do you know how much Jesus loves you? How does His love compel you or motivate you? Are you willing to live a life of risk and openness in being a minister of reconciliation?*

# REAL REALITY: SCRIPTURE MEDITATION

*BELIEVE IT. IT'S TRUE, AND TRUE FOR YOU. AMEN!*

*For Christ's love compels us, because we are convinced that one died for all, and therefore all died.  II Cor. 5:14*

*Therefore, if anyone is in Christ, he is a new creation; the old has gone, the new has come! All this is from God, who reconciled us to himself in Christ, not counting men's sins against them. And he has committed to us the message of reconciliation. We are therefore Christ's ambassadors, as though God were making his appeal through us. We implore you on Christ's behalf: Be reconciled to God! God made Him who knew no sin to be sin for us, so that in him we might become the righteousness of God. II Corinthians 5:17-21*

# Reality Christianity:
# Radiating Christ in Our Cracked Lives

## Week 6: II Corinthians 5:11-6:13

*The Reality of Brokenness / The Reality of our Reconciling God*

*How can you keep a "wide-open" heart in a broken-down, hurting world?*

## MOTIVATION The Mystery of the Double Reality: Fear and Love
## II Corinthians 5:9-15

*What motivates you?* Paul reveals his double motivation for his God-pleasing ministry to those whose hearts seemed closed to him: the fear of the Lord (5:11) and the love of Christ (5:14). He lives in the mysterious reality of a God who is omnipotent and imminent, totally "other" and totally present as our Abba Father. He sees Jesus as Judge (5:10) and judged (5:21). "How is it possible to be motivated by the fear of the Lord and the love of Christ? Are not fear and love irreconcilable? It all depends on a proper understanding of fear and love, which, it should be noted, are not opposites . . .In the Bible, 'fear' is not cringing terror but holy reverence, and 'love' is not romantic feelings but sacrificial care . . .the fear of the Lord and awareness of the love of Christ fit perfectly together to provide the true motivation for Christian ministry."[49]

*The Fear of the Lord:* (5:9-11) Paul begins with the motivation of *fear* (reverence, awe, devotion, awareness of fatherly discipline) of the Lord. He anticipates appearing before the judgment seat of Christ. How can you see the double truth of our justification (how God sees us positionally in Jesus Christ) and our sanctification (how we grow to be like Christ by God's transforming grace). Dr. Bob Flayhart says, "This passage encourages us to not minimize the fight step of the waltz. God is not kidding when He calls us to a life of holiness. We are called to pursue a life that is pleasing to God. We are pleasing to God in our standing, in our position, but our attitudes and actions are either objectively pleasing or displeasing to God in accordance with Scripture. In addition, God says those kinds of things to drive us back to Christ as our only comfort and hope in life and in death. Rather than getting under performance, such verses should push us to the cross for encouragement and hope for transformation. In a word, it's another mystery. Justification is true and sanctification matters!" R. C. Sproul shows the distinction between believers and nonbelievers facing the judgment seat of Christ: "There is no condemnation for those who are in Christ Jesus. (Rom. 8:1). So those who are in Christ need not have any fear of ever having to face the punitive wrath of God in the final judgment . . .But we still must face what I would call the judgment

---

49  Paul Barnett, *The Message of 2 Corinthians* (Inter-Varsity Press: Downers Grove, IL, 1988), 108.

of evaluation. Jesus warns again and again that everything we do, whether we're believers or nonbelievers, will be brought into judgment. I will stand before God, and my life will be reviewed by my Father. Obviously my sins will be covered by the atonement and righteousness of Christ (II Cor. 5:21), and I will have the supreme advantage of standing at the judgment throne of God, where Christ is the judge and also the defense attorney for his people."[50] Warren Wiersbe adds, "Because of the gracious work of Christ on the cross, believers will not face their sins (Rom. 8:1, John 5:24) but we will have to give an account of our works and service for the Lord. The judgment seat of Christ will be a place of revelation. The character of our service will be revealed (I Cor. 3:13) as well as the motives that impelled us (I Cor. 4:5). If we have been faithful, it will be a place of reward and recognition (I Cor. 3:10-15, 4:1-6) and rejoicing as we glorify God by giving our rewards back to Him in worship and in praise. The important thing is not the reward itself, but the joy of pleasing Christ and honoring Him."[51]

*The Love of Christ:* (5:14-15) The love of Christ *compels* us (5:14 NIV) can be interpreted three ways and the order is very important: First, the love of Christ for you (I Jn 4:10). That's the basis of motivation. Second, the love you have for Christ (I Pet. 1:8). Third, the love of Christ flowing from you to others (I John 4:19, I Thes. 2:18, II Cor. 6:11). The Greek work for *compels* (συνεχει) means to hold together, to prevent from falling apart. Positively, it means constraint or compulsion; negatively, it means restraint, like the banks of a river hemming you in.[52] Face this fact, whether you feel it or not: As a believer, you are loved (Rom. 5:5-8, Zeph. 3:17, II Cor. 5:14). "Christ's love is a compulsive force in the life of believers, a dominating power that effectively eradicates choice in that it leaves them no option but to live for God and Christ."[53]

## MINISTRY The Miracle of Reconciliation: Restoration of Relationship II Corinthians 5:16-6:2

*What ministry have you been called to?* Many believers discount that they have a ministry and dismiss their lives as without purpose. These verses give you the roadmap of your ministry, pointing other broken people to the God who reconciles through Jesus Christ. Reconciliation is the restoration of a relationship, the renewal of friendship. Reconciliation is all of God. Even the command to be reconciled to God (5:20) is in passive voice. God reconciles. You receive. Paul states that **you are an ambassador of reconciliation.** In Roman times, ambassadors were sent to imperial provinces, dangerous places prone to rebellion. You represent Jesus Christ in a rebellious, broken world. This ministry only occurs with a

---

50  R. C. Sproul, *Now That's A Good Question* (Wheaton, IL: Tyndale House, 1996), 501.

51  Warren Wiersbe, *Be Encouraged* (Colorado Springs, CO: Chariot Victor Publishing, 1984), 61.

52  Murray J. Harris, *The Second Epistle to the Corinthians* (Eerdmans Publishing Co: Grand Rapids, MI, 2005), 419.

53  Harris, 419.

radical change (5:17) as you receive Christ. You are not called to turn over a new leaf, but to a new life as a new creation. Because of sin, the whole world is broken and alienated from God. God provides, in his mercy and justice, the only solution, a solution that demonstrates his sacrificial love for you. Oswald Chambers says, "Sin is a fundamental relationship; it is not wrong *doing*, it is wrong *being*, deliberate and emphatic independence of God. The Christian religion bases everything on the radical nature of sin. Other religions deal with sins; the Bible alone deals with sin. . . God made His own Son to be sin that He might make the sinner a saint. All through the Bible it is revealed that Our Lord bore the sin of the world by identification, not by *sympathy*. He deliberately took upon His own shoulders, and bore in His own Person, the whole massed sin of the human race—'He hath made Him to be sin for us, who knew no sin' and by so doing He put the whole human race on the basis of Redemption. Jesus Christ rehabilitated the human race; He put it back to where God designed it to be, and anyone can enter into union with God on the ground of what Our Lord has done on the Cross." [54]

II Cor. 5:21 is "one of the most important verses in all of Scripture for understanding the meaning of the atonement and justification. Here we see that the one **who knew no sin** is Jesus Christ and that **he** (God) **made him** (Christ) **to be sin** (*hamartia*, 'sin'). This means that God the Father made Christ to be *regarded and treated* as 'sin' even though Christ himself never sinned (Heb. 4:15; Gal. 3:13). Further, we see that God did this **for our sake**—that is, God regarded and treated 'our' sin (the sin of all who would believe in Christ) as if our sin belonged not to us but to Christ himself. Thus Christ 'died for all' (5:14) and, as Peter wrote, 'He himself bore our sins in his body on the tree' (1 Pet. 2:24). In becoming sin 'for our sake,' Christ became our substitute—that is, Christ took our sin upon himself and, as our substitute, thereby bore the wrath of God (the punishment that we deserve) in our place ('for our sake'). The background for this is Isaiah 53. In a precise fulfillment of this prophecy, Christ became 'sin' for those who believe in him, **so that in him we might become the righteousness of God**. This means that just as God imputed our sin and guilt to Christ ('he made him to be sin') so God also imputes the righteousness of Christ—a righteousness that is not our own—to all who believe in Christ. Because Christ bore the sins of those who believe, God *regards and treats* believers as having the legal status of 'righteousness' (*dikaiosynē*). This righteousness belongs to believers because they are 'in him,' that is, 'in Christ.' Therefore "the righteousness of God" (which is imputed to believers) is also the righteousness of Christ—that is, the righteousness and the legal status that belongs to Christ as a result of Christ having lived as one who 'knew no sin.' This then is the heart of the doctrine of *justification*: God *regards* (or *counts*) believers as forgiven and God *declares* and *treats* them as forgiven, because God the Father has imputed the believer's sin to Christ and because God the Father likewise imputes Christ's righteousness to the believer." [55]

Paul then urges the Corinthians to respond and receive salvation this day. (6:2)

---

54 Oswald Chambers, *My Utmost for His Highest* (Uhrichsville, OH: Barbour), Oct. 7 entry.

55 *ESV Study Bible*, Notes on II Cor. 5:21

## METHOD The Courage to Be Real: Live a Life of Risk and Openness
## II Corinthians 6:3-13

*How can you keep a wide-open heart in a broken-down world with narrow-minded people?* Paul reveals his wounded, bleeding, pouring-out, wide-open heart amid external trials, personal troubles, and inner torment. He gives a manual for all ambassadors of Christ. The key word is the first in his list, **endurance** (6:4). "Endurance amidst adversities is the overarching quality of authentic ministry. This is because the natural inclination is to flee the conflicts of ministry."[56] Some of the Corinthians thought his suffering disqualified him for successful ministry. He still endured. "So often our words are ignored by others, including our nearest and dearest. But when they observe endurance for Christ in the midst of showers of troubles, they cannot deny the reality of our faith in Christ . . .his endurance rests in his purity of motive and life, in Spirit-given knowledge of Christ himself, in a Spirit-imbued patience that is not provoked to anger, in a genuine, unhypocritical love, in truthful speech, and in the power of God."[57]

Read II Cor. 6:4-13 in *The Message*: "People are watching us as we stay at our post, alertly, unswervingly . . . in hard times, tough times, bad times; when we're beaten up, jailed, and mobbed; working hard, working late, working without eating; with pure heart, clear head, steady hand; in gentleness, holiness, and honest love; when we're telling the truth, and when God's showing his power; when we're doing our best setting things right; when we're praised, and when we're blamed; slandered, and honored; true to our word, though distrusted; ignored by the world, but recognized by God; terrifically alive, though rumored to be dead; beaten within an inch of our lives, but refusing to die; immersed in tears, yet always filled with deep joy; living on handouts, yet enriching many; having nothing, having it all. Dear, dear Corinthians, I can't tell you how much I long for you to enter this wide-open, spacious life. We didn't fence you in. The smallness you feel comes from within you. Your lives aren't small, but you're living them in a small way. I'm speaking as plainly as I can and with great affection. Open up your lives. Live openly and expansively!"

A. W. Tozer, in *That Incredible Christian*, describes **this paradoxical Christian life**, "The Christian believes that in Christ he has died, yet he is more alive than before and he fully expects to live forever. . .He loses his life to save it and is in danger of losing it if he attempts to preserve it. . .He is strongest when he is weakest and weakest when he is strong. Though poor he has the power to make others rich, but when he becomes rich his ability to enrich others vanishes. . .He may be and often is highest when he feels lowest and most sinless when he is most conscious of sin. . .He sometimes does most by doing nothing and goes furthest when standing still. . He fears God but is not afraid of Him. In God's presence he feels overwhelmed and undone, yet there is nowhere he would rather be than in that presence."[58]

---

56  R. Kent Hughes, *2 Corinthians: Power in Weakness* (Crossway Books: Wheaton, IL, 2006), 132.

57  Hughes, 134

58  Ray C. Stedman, *Authentic Christianity* (Discovery House Publishers: Grand Rapids, MI, 1996), 137.

## Meditating on the Love of Christ and God in II Corinthians 5:14 and 5:21

## And Can It Be?

Charles Wesley

And can it be that I should gain
An interest in the Savior's blood?
Died He for me, who caused His pain—
For me, who Him to death pursued?
Amazing love! How can it be,
That Thou, my God, shouldst die for me?
Amazing love! How can it be,
That Thou, my God, shouldst die for me?

'Tis mystery all: th'Immortal dies:
Who can explore His strange design?
In vain the firstborn seraph tries
To sound the depths of love divine.
'Tis mercy all! Let earth adore,
Let angel minds inquire no more.
'Tis mercy all! Let earth adore;
Let angel minds inquire no more.

He left His Father's throne above
So free, so infinite His grace—
Emptied Himself of all but love,
And bled for Adam's helpless race:
'Tis mercy all, immense and free,
For O my God, it found out me!
'Tis mercy all, immense and free,
For O my God, it found out me!

Long my imprisoned spirit lay,
Fast bound in sin and nature's night;
Thine eye diffused a quickening ray—
I woke, the dungeon flamed with light;
My chains fell off, my heart was free,
I rose, went forth, and followed Thee.
My chains fell off, my heart was free,
I rose, went forth, and followed Thee.

Still the small inward voice I hear,
That whispers all my sins forgiven;
Still the atoning blood is near,
That quenched the wrath of hostile Heaven.
I feel the life His wounds impart;
I feel the Savior in my heart.
I feel the life His wounds impart;
I feel the Savior in my heart.

No condemnation now I dread;
Jesus, and all in Him, is mine;
Alive in Him, my living Head,
And clothed in righteousness divine,
Bold I approach th'eternal throne,
And claim the crown, through Christ my own.
Bold I approach th'eternal throne,
And claim the crown, through Christ my own.

# Week 7: The Reality of REALationships
## II Corinthians 6:14-7:16

*Questions marked with an * are for those doing Bible Study Express.*

## Day 1: Relationships with Unbelievers

 **Read II Corinthians 6:14-7:1.** What is Paul's main point in these verses?*

What kind of relationships or partnerships is Paul talking about?

What does Paul mean by *yoked?*\*

What does it mean to be in the world and not of it? Have you ever used the command in II Corinthians 6 to isolate yourself from unbelievers?

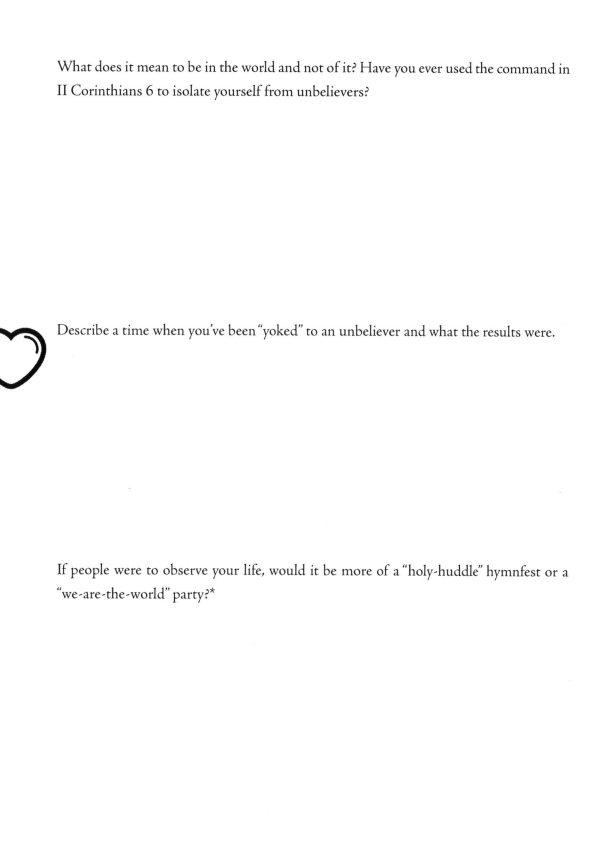

Describe a time when you've been "yoked" to an unbeliever and what the results were.

If people were to observe your life, would it be more of a "holy-huddle" hymnfest or a "we-are-the-world" party?*

Pray for wisdom and balance. Discuss with your group ways you can be separate and holy unto God and yet still reach out to the world?*

Consolidate the message of II Corinthians 6:14-7:16 into one sentence. Share that sentence with a family member, friend, or someone in your group this week.

*Optional: Do discovery sheet on II Corinthians 6:14-7:16 found at the end of the weekly lesson.*

**Read II Corinthians 6:14-7:1.** What attributes of God do you see in these verses?*
What promises does he give?*

According to these verses, write down who you are if you are a believer.*

What is reverence for God?

 What is contaminating your body or spirit?*

Pray that God will give you the light to see and repent of sins, idols, habits, thought patterns, relationships, and use of your time and tongue, and that He will purify you.

 Until you really believe who you are in Christ, (a holy temple, a "chosen people," a son or daughter of the Lord Almighty), you won't be able to "fight" for holiness in your life. Right now, fight to believe who you are in Christ. If you are not sure you are a believer, take time to honestly talk to God about your sin, your inability to fix it on your own, and your surrender to Jesus Christ as your only hope for salvation and life.

As you believe who you are and God's power in you and promises to you, then you can begin to fight. Name practical ways that you will, by God's grace, separate yourself from specific sins and become more like Him.*

**Read II Corinthians 7:2-16.** Also read Matthew 27:3-5. What is the difference between worldly sorrow and godly sorrow?* What does worldly sorrow lead to?*

How was Judas an example of worldly sorrow? What could he have done to have godly sorrow or true repentance?

 Were you surprised, relieved, concerned, or disappointed to know that Paul had to battle with conflicts, fears, and depression in the midst of his ministry?

Describe a time when you experienced worldly sorrow.*

 Are you willing to go from worldly sorrow to godly sorrow? Ask God to make you aware of areas of your life where you are avoiding "getting real" with God about your sin.*

**Read II Corinthians 7:2-16** and Luke 22:31-34, 54-62 and Psalm 51. In II Corinthians 7:11, what does godly sorrow produce?*

What is real repentance?*

How are David and Peter examples of godly sorrow? How are their responses different from Judas?

Just as you described a time of worldly sorrow, now describe a time when you have had real repentance or godly sorrow.* How was it different from worldly sorrow?

 True repentance is a gift! *God's kindness leads you toward repentance. Romans 2:4* As you have been going through this study and reading Scripture, where has God been leading you to repentance which leads to life?

Spend time asking God to make you truly aware of your sins in a way that will make you turn away from them and to God.*

**Read II Corinthians 7:2-16.** What is Paul's goal with the Corinthians?*

Describe Paul's emotions and actions and the Corinthians' response.

How can Paul's use of encouragement and exhortation be applied to how you relate to those you desire to grow in the Lord?

What principles of redemptive relationships can you apply from Jesus' restoring of Peter in John 21:15-19 and from Paul's dealing with the Corinthians?

Share a time when someone who really loved you has told you a hard truth about yourself and how that made you feel.

As you think of conflicts you have with loved ones (or not-so-loved ones!), check your heart. What is your goal and desire in the situation? Is it to:

_____be proved right

_____for justice to be served

_____make the problem go away

_____deal with it so you never have to go there again

_____be redemptive and restorative?

What is your desire for the person you are having conflict with?*

Rethink your relationships, especially those closest to you. Repent of "it's-all-about-me" focus and ask God to begin developing a deep, Christ-focused love for others where you are willing to enter into a REALationship with the goal of true Christ-revealing growth for both of you.

# OPTIONAL PERSONAL DISCOVERY SHEET

II Corinthians 6:14-7:16

## CONTENT

List the main points from this Scripture.

## DIVISIONS

Divide content into 2-4 main sections and write a sentence for each division.

## ESSENCE OF PASSAGE

Write a short sentence (10 words or less!) that gives the thrust of the passage.

## ESSENTIAL QUESTION/AIM

Write the main "transformational truth" to remember from studying this Scripture. Make this as short and simple as possible. It helps to put it in the form of a question to link it to application.

## APPLICATIONS

Write specific questions or challenges to help put the aim into action or answer the question. Are there specific areas in which you need to repent? To believe God and his Word? To live out and apply the gospel?

# Week 7: The Reality of REALationships and the Reality of Our Redemptive God
## II Corinthians 6:14-7:16

## GROUP DISCUSSION

✓ *Does thinking about living a life of holiness and repentance fill you with longing and hope or dread and defeat? Why?*

✓ *If you really believed who you are and whose you are, how would you fight for yourself and others differently?*

✓ *Where do you need to get in or stay in the "beautiful mess" of redemptive relationships?*

## TEACHING TIME

*Stay in the Real Fight: Remember Who You Are So You Can:*

### I. LIVE A LIFE OF:

*Since/then: Since as a believer, you are beloved and belong to God, then you can focus on the real fight for holy living.*

### II. LIVE A LIFE OF:

*Repentance is a lifestyle of letting go of our idols and coming to Jesus Christ. It is a great gift and reality check that God is real and cares about our lives.*

## III. LIVE A LIFE OF:

*Bless this mess! We're called to redemptive relationships. It is worth it.*

## REALITY CHECK

*How can you remember who you really are and whose you are, so that you'll stay in the real fight: To live reverently, repentantly, and redemptively in a hard and unholy world filled with bruised and broken people?*

## REAL REALITY: SCRIPTURE MEDITATION

*BELIEVE IT. IT'S TRUE, AND TRUE FOR YOU. AMEN!*

*Since we have these promises, **beloved,** let us cleanse ourselves from every defilement of body and spirit, bringing holiness to completion in the fear of God. II Corinthians 7:1*

*Remember who you are, who God is and, what He is doing: If you are a believer, you are a righteous, light-filled temple of the living God, one of His people and His son and daughter. He is the Living God, the Lord Almighty, our Reconciling and Redeeming God. He is the God who comforts the downcast and leads us to repentance. He promises to live with us and walk with us and be our God and we will be His people. He will be a Father to us and we will be His children. Because of His passion for His glory and our holiness and wholeness in Him, he will lead us to a life of ongoing reverence of Him, repentance, and redemption.*

# Reality Christianity:
# Radiating Christ in Our Cracked Lives

## Week 7: II Corinthians 6:14-7:16

*The Reality of REALationships / The Reality of our Redeeming God*

## Pick Your Fight: Know What the Real Battle Is
## II Corinthians 6:14-7:16

What lessons we can learn from Paul in loving his troubled spiritual children, in calling them to be who they really are, in longing for their lives to be whole and holy, for being honest with his inner struggles, for getting into the risk of real relationships, and rejoicing over the good reports? As believers, we live in this "beautiful mess" of a world filled with brokenness and hope, the double reality of being a saint and a sinner in relationships with other sinning saints. Paul is calling the Corinthians to live reverent, repentant lives and to be involved in redemptive relationships. He knows the real battle is to remember and really believe who they are in Christ.

We are at the end of Paul's long interruption (2:14-7:4) where he speaks of his anxiety in waiting in Macedonia (can't you picture him pacing back and forth) for word of Titus and the reception of his severe letter. In this detour, Paul defends "reality Christianity" through his own life, the Corinthians' lives and, most importantly, Jesus Christ. Real Christianity is all about Jesus Christ radiating his fragrance (2:15) and light (4:6) through our cracked lives (4:7). It is not about success, but about submission (2:14), not about competence but new covenant living (3:5-6). It's about being compelled by his love (5:14) and being ambassadors of reconciliation (5:20) and completing holiness (7:1) in fear of the Lord. In 7:5-9 Paul reveals his outer and inner conflicts as he waits in Macedonia and rejoices in the God of comfort sending Titus to Timothy and him with the good report. In chapter 7, Paul reveals what real repentance is and role models a redemptive relationship. In chapters 8-9, he calls these repentant believers to complete the giving and in the 10-13 his tone changes again to warn the unrepentant.

## Stay in the Fight: Live a Life of Reverence
## II Corinthians 6:14-7:1

Paul's commands follow a pattern: when he calls believers to do something, he reminds them who they are in Christ. Here Paul calls the Corinthians to be separate and holy because of their intimate relationship to the Living God. He begins by warning them not to be unequally yoked. This image is taken from Deut. 22:10's command to not plow with an ox and donkey. They could not keep pace with each other and possibly would kill each other. "It is an image for being allied or identified wrongly with unbelievers. In context, it refers especially to those who are still rebelling against Paul within the church, whom Paul now shockingly labels unbelievers . . . but the principle has wider application to other situations where (as with animals yoked together) one person's conduct and direction of life strongly influences or controls the other's."[59] In Matthew 11:28-30, we learn who we are to be yoked with: *Come to me, all who labor and are heavy laden, and I will give you rest. Take my yoke upon you, and _learn from me, for I am gentle and lowly in heart, and you will find rest for your souls. For my yoke is easy, and my burden is light.* Christ invites us to come and keep pace with him in his work which will give soul rest. Paul then shows them who they are (righteous, light, believers, temple of God, sons and daughters of God) and whose they are (God's people, God's children, His beloved) and who God is (Christ, living God, the Lord Almighty) as he calls them to be separated, let go of their idols, and to perfect or complete their holiness in the fear of the Lord. Paul gives them promises from six Old Testament quotations to reinforce his call for holiness. "Paul emphasizes two promises that were made as part of Israel's promised deliverance from bondage . . . a promise of personal *intimacy* (6:16) and a promise of personal *adoption* (6:18) . . . The Corinthians were full beneficiaries of the new covenant's deliverance and restoration. And as such, they should pursue separation and holiness."[60] In 7:1, Paul begins with "since." We do not live in an *if/then* performance world with God. Because of Jesus Christ, we live in a *since/then* grace world. Because of Jesus Christ, we have been reconciled to our God as living God and loving Father, so we are His beloved and so that Paul can state with confidence to become who they really are: *Since we have these promises, beloved, let us cleanse ourselves from every defilement of body and spirit, bringing holiness to completion in the fear of God.*

## Stay in the Fight: Live a Life of Repentance
## II Corinthians 7:2-16

In the rest of chapter 7, Paul reveals the depth of his emotions as he awaited Titus' return to Macedonia and the Corinthians response to his severe letter. Although grieved he does not regret sending the reprimanding letter because of how the Corinthians responded in godly grief, in a repentance that has no regrets and leads to life. Paul distinguishes between worldly sorrow which leads to death and godly grief which brings life. *Worldly sorrow* "is a grief for oneself, centered on self, not grief for sin against God. It grieves over consequences. It aches with embarrassment. It focuses on its own hurt. It is self-pitying."[61] *Godly grief* "is a grief that comes from knowing your actions are unpleasing to God . . . such a grief is 'blessed' because it drives us to God and to repentance."[62] It is David's cry in Psalm 51: *For I know my transgressions, and my sin is ever before me. Against you, you only, have I sinned and done what is evil in*

---

59 *ESV Study Bible*, Notes on II Cor. 6:14

60 R. Kent Hughes, *2 Corinthians: Power in Weakness* (Crossway Books: Wheaton, IL, 2006), 143.

61 Hughes, 151.

62 Hughes, 151.

*your sight.* You are undone and turn away from your sin and to God. It is God's gift of kindness which leads you to repentance (Romans 2:4) and although painful, is a beautiful reminder that we are His children and He will restore us. In a world filled with half-hearted apologies and rationalizing remorse over being caught, when we see a truly repentant person offering no excuses and humble enough to ask for forgiveness and help, we know that it is of God. Repentance and faith are the entry points into a lifestyle of ongoing repentance and faith.

## Stay in the Fight:  Live a Life of Redemptive Relationships
## II Corinthians 7:2-16

"Bless this mess." Deeply redemptive, restoring relationships are messy and painful. Thank God for our *Mess*iah who continues to save us in our messes. We are called to love others in the way Paul pursues the Corinthians: with vulnerability, courage to speak truth in love, pray and keep our hearts open even when rejected or wounded, and always have a God-vision and confidence of who they (and we) are becoming. Those who help the most are those who remember who they are now and who they were in their mess, who can live in the tension of being part of a group of sinning saints and are compelled by his love to love his other children. Think of Peter who Jesus restored to ministry after he betrayed him. Jesus called him to love his sheep.

What about you?  Are you willing to get in the beautiful mess of life? "Our eyes need to be open and our hearts generous with compassionate care. Above all we must resist the temptation to run away from people's needs because we do not think we can cope. The troubled do not usually expect us to solve their problems; but they do appreciate our concern and prayerful support. What matters most to people in distress is not 'saying things' but 'being there.'"[63] Are you willing to be there in the mess and fight as His beloved for wholeness and holiness in broken people, including yourself?

---

63  Paul Barnett, *The Message of 2 Corinthians* (Inter-Varsity Press:  Downers Grove, IL, 1988), 108.

# Week 8: The Reality of Reaping
## II Corinthians 8:1-9:15

*Questions marked with an * are for those doing "Bible Study Express."*

## Day 1: Real Grace Giving

**Read II Corinthians 8:1-15.** Paul uses II Corinthians 8 and 9 to encourage the Corinthians in the grace of giving. Macedonia, north of Corinth, included the churches at Philippi, Thessalonica, and Berea. We often focus on *what* is given. Paul focuses on *how* it is given. From this passage, describe *how* the Macedonians gave.*

Who was Paul collecting money for and why? (See also Acts 11:27-30, Romans 15:26-27)

What does Paul mean when he exhorts the Corinthians to *"excel in the grace of giving?"*

Have you known anyone who is filled with joy and gives despite their dire financial circumstances or other hardships? Why do you think he or she was able to give with joy?

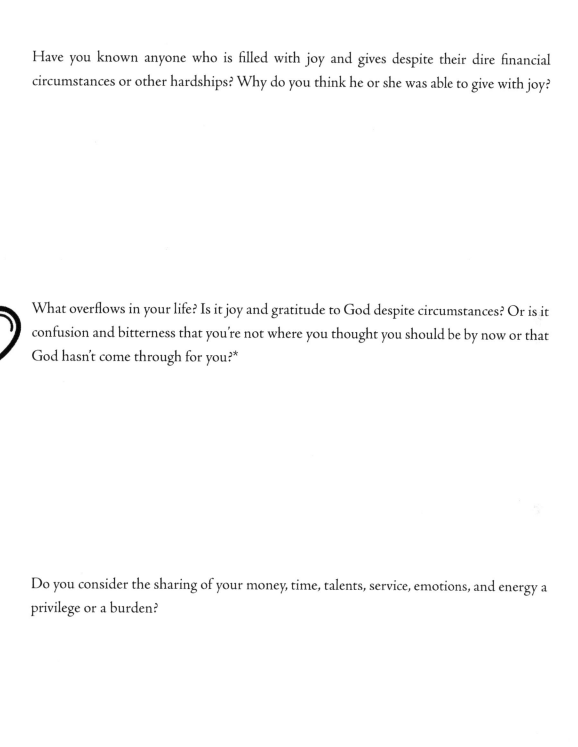

What overflows in your life? Is it joy and gratitude to God despite circumstances? Or is it confusion and bitterness that you're not where you thought you should be by now or that God hasn't come through for you?*

Do you consider the sharing of your money, time, talents, service, emotions, and energy a privilege or a burden?

Describe a time when you have experienced the "grace of giving."

 The Holy Spirit, through Paul, convicts not about giving but also in following through and finishing what you've started. Share with your group a project or commitment you've been avoiding finishing that has been weighing on you. Ask them to pray with you that by God's grace you will finish well and be free.*

Consolidate the message of II Corinthians 8:1-9:15 into one sentence. Share that sentence with a family member, friend, or someone in your group this week.

*Optional: Do discovery sheet on II Corinthians 8:1-9:15 found at the end of the weekly lesson.*

**Read II Corinthians 8:1-15.** Also read Philippians 2:9-11 and Romans 5:6-11. What does Paul mean when he says that Christ "became poor" for our sakes?*

Relish the riches of Christ. Describe how Jesus Christ is rich from this passage and from other Bible references.

How have we been made rich?*

Explain Paul's equality principle (vs. 13-15). Do you see that at work in our culture?

Describe a time when you have felt "rich" in Christ.*

As you look at the world, do you really want true equality and fairness? As you examine your own heart, do you often compare yourself with others and feel that God hasn't been fair to you?

 They say there's nothing like examining your checkbook, pocketbook, and datebook to get a reality check of your spiritual life. If Paul were to "test the sincerity of your love" for Christ (II Cor. 8:8), how would you grade yourself? Do this not as a guilt trip, but as a way of repentance and renewal and prayer. How can your group pray for you this week?*

**Read II Corinthians 8:16-9:5.** What is the main concern Paul and Titus have for the Corinthians?*

What were some ways in which Paul was very careful in how he asked for, collected, and distributed the collection?

*Freely you have received. Freely give. Matthew 10:8.* Do you give freely or fearfully?

How freely do you receive from God and others?*

Do you always think you have to earn it before you receive it?

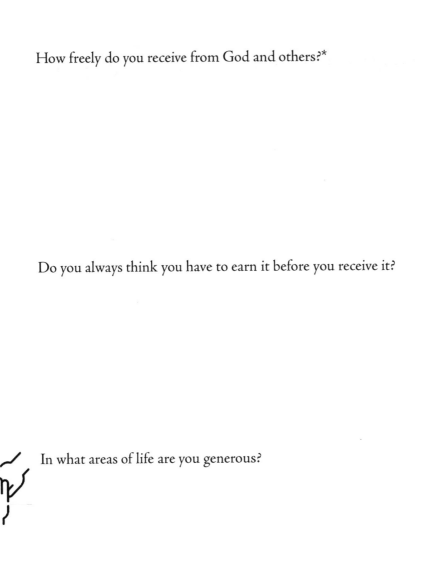 In what areas of life are you generous?

Where are you miserly or have a hoarding spirit?

As you look at the areas of life where you hold on tightly, what is it that you most fear?

Repent of areas of fear and unbelief and pray that you will begin to experience freedom in both receiving and giving.*

**Read II Corinthians 9:6-15.** Restate the "Reaping Principle" in II Corinthians 9:6 in your own words.*

Does Paul mean in II Corinthians 9:6 that you can expect a good return on your "investment?" Explain your answer.

What is God's indescribable gift?*

Where are you a cheerful giver and where are you a calculating giver?

How do you deal with your reluctant heart in regards to giving of yourself or your money for the good of God's people and His Kingdom's work?*

 Ask God to give you a glance at your own heart about giving. Ask your group to pray for you in a specific area where you need to trust Him to be a cheerful giver (of your money, time, talent, energy, emotions, home, possessions, or your spouse's or loved one's time).*

**Read II Corinthians 9:6-15.** What attributes and promises of God do you see in these verses?*

Read II Corinthians 9:8 carefully. List all the "alls" and "every."

Is God able to know and provide for all your "alls"?

How is giving contagious?

What benefits does our giving produce in others?

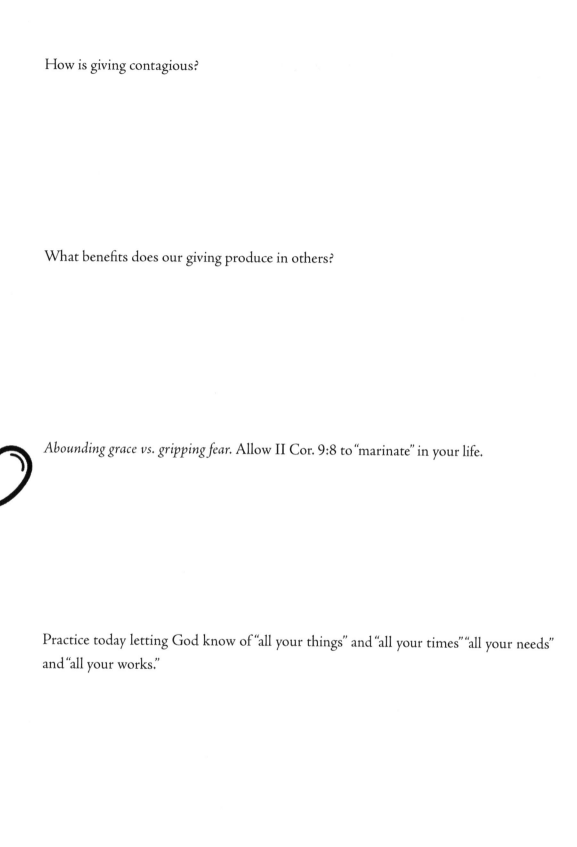 *Abounding grace vs. gripping fear.* Allow II Cor. 9:8 to "marinate" in your life.

Practice today letting God know of "all your things" and "all your times" "all your needs" and "all your works."

Meditate afresh on His indescribable gift.

Write down and share with your group times you have experienced God's abounding grace in your life.

 Today, by faith, believe and fight to believe God's promises and his gift. Write a thank you note to God for his indescribable gift to you.

# OPTIONAL PERSONAL DISCOVERY SHEET

II Corinthians 8:1-9:15

## CONTENT

List the main points from this Scripture.

## DIVISIONS

Divide content into 2-4 main sections and write a sentence for each division.

## ESSENCE OF PASSAGE

Write a short sentence (10 words or less!) that gives the thrust of the passage.

## ESSENTIAL QUESTION/AIM

Write the main "transformational truth" to remember from studying this Scripture. Make this as short and simple as possible. It helps to put it in the form of a question to link it to application.

## APPLICATIONS

Write specific questions or challenges to help put the aim into action or answer the question. Are there specific areas in which you need to repent? To believe God and his Word? To live out and apply the gospel?

## *Week 8: The Reality of Reaping and the Reality of Our  Enriching God*
## II Corinthians 8:1-9:15

---

## GROUP DISCUSSION

✓  What difference has grace made in your life?

## TEACHING TIME

### GRACE AS RECEIVING
### II Corinthians 8-9

*GRACE AS SUPERNATURAL INTERVENTION, GOD'S UNMERITED FAVOR*

### WHAT QUESTIONS SHOULD YOU ASK?

✓  Who is God? What has He done and what is He doing?

✓  Who is Christ? What has He done and what is He doing?

✓  Who are you? What has God done, what is He enabling you to do and what is your struggle?

### GRACE AS RESPONDING
### II Corinthians  8-9

*GRACE AS SUPERNATURAL POWER, GOD'S ENABLING POWER*

NOT "IF/THEN" BUT "SINCE/THEN"

THE EXAMPLE OF THE MACEDONIANS:

THE REAPING PRINCIPLE

GOD'S PROMISES AND BLESSINGS

## REALITY CHECK

*Where does God most need to transform you so that you can give freely and not fearfully or grudgingly?*

## REAL REALITY: SCRIPTURE MEDITATION

*BELIEVE IT. IT'S TRUE, AND TRUE FOR YOU. AMEN!*

*For you know the grace of our Lord Jesus Christ, that though he was rich, yet for your sakes he became poor, so that you through his poverty might become rich. II Corinthians 8:9*

*And God is able to make all grace abound to you, so that in all things at all times, having all that you need, you will abound in every good work. II Corinthians 9:8*

*Thanks be to God for His indescribable gift. II Corinthians 9:15*

As a believer, you have been given the indescribable gift of salvation and reconciliation to God through Jesus Christ. You are rich and have abounding, surpassing, enabling grace which will overflow in a thankful, joyful generous life that glorifies God and gives to others.

*Hymn to mediate on following this lesson*

# When I Survey the Wondrous Cross

By Isaac Watts


When I survey the wondrous cross
On which the Prince of glory died,
My richest gain I count but loss,
And pour contempt on all my pride.


Forbid it, Lord, that I should boast,
Save in the death of Christ my God!
All the vain things that charm me most,
I sacrifice them to His blood.


See from His head, His hands, His feet,
Sorrow and love flow mingled down!
Did e'er such love and sorrow meet,
Or thorns compose so rich a crown?


Were the whole realm of nature mine,
That were a present far too small;
**Love so amazing, so divine,**
**Demands my soul, my life, my all.**

# Reality Christianity:
# Radiating Christ in Our Cracked Lives

## Week 8: II Corinthians 8:1-9:15

*The Reality of Reaping / The Reality of Our Enriching God*

## Grace: How will you RSVP?

At first glance, II Corinthians 8-9 is all about giving. But if you read it carefully you see that it is all about grace: recognizing it, receiving it, responding to it. Grace (*charis*) appear eight times in these two chapters. Other similar words (gift, privilege/favor, generous, give, thanksgiving) appear 15 times. The acronym for grace, "God's Riches at Christ's Expense" flow right from II Corinthians 8:9 *For you know the grace of our Lord Jesus Christ, that though he was rich, yet for your sake he became poor, so that you by his poverty might become rich.*

Stop now and put your name in that verse: *For you know the grace of our Lord Jesus Christ, that though he was rich, yet for* _____ *sake he became poor, so that* _____ *by his poverty might become rich.*

Have you recognized that you are really that poor without Jesus Christ? Have you trusted in Christ alone for your salvation and every part of your life and journey? If so, do you believe you are that rich?

These chapters give you a reality check on how grace has truly affected your life. First, how well do you receive? Especially when you can't pay it back? And you can never pay back God.

Second, how do you give? Are you a calculating giver or a cheerful extravagant giver? It's based on where you think the resources are coming from and whose they are.

Third, do you live a grumbling or grateful life? Is your default mode one of suspicion, resentment, and grasping or trust, freedom, and releasing?

For this lesson, we're going to start at the end: *Thanks be to God for his inexpressible gift.* (9:15) "This is the first time the Greek word translated 'inexpressible' appears anywhere in the Greek language. Paul could find no word to express the ineffable character of God's gift, so he made one up—a word that says, in effect, that the gift can't be described."[64]

---

64 [1]R. Kent Hughes, *2 Corinthians: Power in Weakness* (Crossway Books: Wheaton, IL, 2006), 176.

How thankful are you for Jesus Christ? Not in a pat, "right" answer way. But in a deep daily dependent way. Relish who Jesus Christ is and what he has done for you through Scriptures such as Philippians 2:5-11, Romans 5:6-11 and 8:31-39, II Corinthians 5:21, and Ephesians 3:16-21.

## Grace: Receiving vs. Refusing
## II Corinthians 8:1-15

Paul has reminded the Corinthians who they are in Christ, and that they are to live reverent and repentant lives as God's beloved in II Corinthians 6-7. He has opened wide his heart (6:11) and asked them to open wide their hearts (6:13) and their hands in giving (8:7, 11) to the needs of the Christians in famine-stricken Jerusalem. This collection had begun more than a decade before and has stalled out over the last year as Paul confronts and waits for the response from the repentant Corinthian believers. "Chapters 8-9 relate to what Paul elsewhere calls the. . . 'contribution for the poor among the saints in Jerusalem.' . . .Paul and Barnabas made a missionary compact with the Jerusalem church 'pillars,' James, Peter, and John. It was agreed that James, Peter, and John would evangelize the Jews while Paul and Barnabas would go to the Gentiles. The one condition attaching to this missionary agreement was that Paul and Barnabas should 'remember the poor,' that is, making provision from the Gentile churches for the poor among the Christians in Jerusalem."[65] Paul, receiving the good report from Titus about the Corinthians, focuses them on the grace they've received (8:9) and the grace that makes them able to respond (9:8). Grace is God's supernatural intervention in our lives, reaching down to reconcile us through the death of his son, Jesus Christ, and his ongoing undeserved gracious hand intervening as we receive his acceptance, help and power. Paul uses the Macedonians as an example of grace-responders. They understood the privilege (*charis*) of giving in a beyond-their-ability, begging-to-give kind of way first to the Lord and then to Paul, Titus, and the ministry. "Such is the grace of giving. It is not dictated by ability. It has nothing to do with being well-off. It is willing. It views giving as a privilege. It is joyously enthusiastic."[66] Paul's ultimate example of grace-giving is Jesus Christ (8:9) as he invites us to consider the grace of Jesus Christ in exchanging his infinite riches for our inconceivable poverty. **Thanks be to God for his inexpressible gift!**

## Grace: Giving vs. Grasping
## II Corinthians 8:16-9:5

Paul shows the Corinthians his hands even as he asks them to open their hands. He is a man of integrity and realizes that money can be the great divider. He does double honor: to God, and to his fellow men (8:21). He sends Titus (his soul brother[67]) and two unnamed reputable believing men (the famous brother and the earnest brother[68]) to collect the money. This is not like the Mafia. It is above-and-beyond

---

65 [2] Paul Barnett, *The Message of 2 Corinthians* (Inter-Varsity Press: Downers Grove, IL, 1988), 108.

66 Hughes, 158.

67 Hughes, 165.

68 Hughes, 165-7.

proof of Paul's integrity and their sincerity by their loving obedience to complete their commitment. Grace is about God's powerful hand gripping ours and engulfing us in our inheritance. We no longer, like orphans, need to grasp and hoard for ourselves because we are gripped by his grace. **Thanks be to God for his inexpressible gift!**

## Grace: Gratitude vs. Grumbling
## II Corinthians 9:6-15

Grace is not only God's supernatural intervention reaching down to us. It is his supernatural power flowing through us to transform us. God is able (9:8) "Paul makes clear that this power is available for the Corinthians, not just the Macedonians. . .This is not a health, wealth, and prosperity gospel. The joy the Macedonians had (8:2) was in Christ, not things. Then, after grace gave rise to abundant joy in Christ, love overflowed. This joy 'overflowed in a wealth of generosity' for the poor. And this is not constrained, but free and lavish."[69] Paul shows the Corinthians the 'how' of giving: cheerfully, with overflowing gratitude. Have you ever been the recipient of someone 'forced' to give you something? How have you felt when manipulated to give? God does not manipulate. God desires that his grace would so transform every aspect of our lives that we could live out the reaping principle of sowing bountifully and reaping bountifully.

Paul shows three benefits of giving in these verses:

1. The generous giver will reap a harvest of righteousness. "The greater the giving, the greater the enrichment. The greater the enrichment the greater resources to give."[70] The paradox of II Corinthians is again seen. "We receive in order to give, not in order to hoard. . . Enrichment of every kind leads to, or leaves the way open for, generosity of every kind."[71]

2. Their giving will overflow with gratitude to God and is a proof (not the basis) of their salvation.

3. Their giving will "establish a bond of affection and prayer between giver and receiver." Think of it as a grace "chain reaction of generosity, thanksgiving, and fellowship. Hence, Paul thanks God for his indescribable gift (9:15), Jesus Christ, which has begun it all."[72]

Again we say: **Thanks be to God for his inexpressible gift!**

---

69 John Piper, *When I Don't Desire God: How to Fight for Joy* (Crossways Books: Wheaton, IL, 2004), 141.

70 Barnett, 154.

71 Murray J. Harris, *The Second Epistle to the Corinthians* (Eerdmans Publishing Co: Grand Rapids, MI, 2005), 645.

72 Barnett, 155.

# Week 9: The Reality of Spiritual Warfare
## II Corinthians 10

*Questions marked with an * are for those doing "Bible Study Express."*

## Day 1: The Real War Paul Faced and We Face

 **Read II Corinthians 10:1-18.** Paul's message to the Corinthians does not change, but beginning in II Corinthians 10, his tone does. In chapters 1-7, Paul calls the Corinthians to be obedient to his apostolic authority and his tone is more encouraging and gentle. In chapters 8-9, Paul reminds the Corinthians what they have received and how they should respond. In chapters 10-13, Paul goes on the attack against the false teachers ("super apostles" in II Corinthians 11:5) who were distracting and dividing the church. It is helpful to read these last four chapters as a unit to get a clearer picture of the unity of Paul's message, his heart for Christ's glory and the church, and his vulnerability about his own life.

What is Paul urgently appealing the Corinthians to be aware of and do in this chapter?*

What attributes of Christ does Paul emphasize in verse 1 and why?*

Read I Corinthians 2:1-5. What is Paul's heart and method of ministry? Contrast his motivation and method with those who are trying to discredit him.

Paul is calling for us to be discerning, especially in spiritual matters. How can you develop discernment?

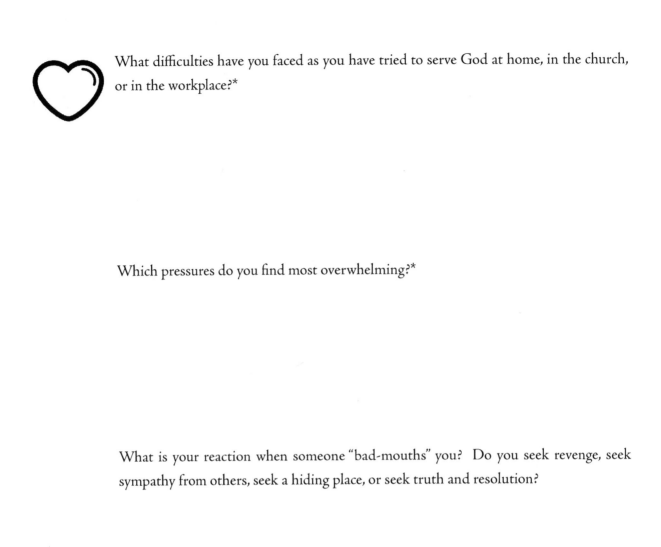

What difficulties have you faced as you have tried to serve God at home, in the church, or in the workplace?*

Which pressures do you find most overwhelming?*

What is your reaction when someone "bad-mouths" you? Do you seek revenge, seek sympathy from others, seek a hiding place, or seek truth and resolution?

How can you be a minister of reconciliation (II Corinthians 5:18) in this kind of personal attack?

Paul comes out fighting in II Corinthians 10. What do you fight for? How do you know when to fight and how to fight? List some things you would be willing to fight for.*

Consolidate the message of II Corinthians 10 into one sentence. Share that sentence with a family member, friend, or someone in your group this week.

*Optional: Do discovery sheet on II Corinthians 10 found at the end of the weekly lesson.*

**Read II Corinthians 10:1-11.** Also read Ephesians 6:10-18 and Colossians 2:13-15. From these passages, what is Paul's strategy in spiritual warfare?*

From II Corinthians 10:3-6, contrast worldly ways with divine power. Think of a specific conflict or issue and describe the different ways it could be addressed from a worldly point of view and a divine point of view.

Paul has called for us to be discerning and know what to fight for and when to fight. What weapons are we to fight with?

How have you been fighting your battles like the world does? Give an example of a battle where you've used spiritual strategies.*

The "comparison game" is one of the world's most subtle and effective weapons. Paul's ministry was affected by it. Where have you played the "comparison game" in how you look at yourself, your spouse, children, friends, church members, ministers, and fellow workers?

What affect has it had on them and on you?

Where have you been wounded by people comparing you to others?

 This is a call-to-fight chapter. Think of a "war" or struggle you are in right now. Have you been fighting with spiritual weapons? What weapons do you need to use?

Ask your group to pray for you in this battle.*

**Read II Corinthians 10:1-11.** Because the spiritual battle is often fought in our own minds, renew your mind by thinking about the words Paul uses to describe the battleground. Define these words:*

Divine Power

Strongholds

Arguments

Pretensions

Take Captive

Obedience to Christ

Which of your thoughts do you need to take captive and make obedient to Christ?

Where are you discouraged or defeated and feel like you are losing the battle?

Where have you found divine power to help you in your thought-life battle?*

 Begin exercising! Practice this day (okay, try it for five minutes first!) to capture every thought and make it obedient to Christ.*

**Read II Corinthians 10:1-18.** What does it mean to *boast in the Lord?**

What is the source of Paul's power and authority in ministry?*

How have he and the church been hurt by these false teachers?

Leadership is hard work and can be more difficult in a "Christian" setting because you're not just dealing with people but with spiritual forces. How can you be both strong and gentle in your leadership roles at home and in the church?

 Write down ways you can practice the meekness, gentleness, and divine power of Christ in one important relationship in your life.*

**Read II Corinthians 10: 12-18.** What is Paul's hope?

What is his desire or goal?*

What is Paul's missionary strategy? (Also read Romans 15:20-24.)

Why is Paul so eager to see the Corinthians grow into a strong church?

 Read II Corinthians 10:8. In your relationships and ministry, where are you building up?

Where are you tearing down?*

How sensitive are you to "turf" issues?

How do you react when someone else receives credit for work you did or ideas you came up with?

 Are you willing to expand beyond your boundaries? If God calls you, can you let others continue building on what you've started, so that you may be used in a new way or with a different group of people? Ask your group to pray for you to be open and listening for God's call on your life and role in His Kingdom.*

# OPTIONAL PERSONAL DISCOVERY SHEET

II Corinthians 10

## CONTENT

List the main points from this Scripture.

## DIVISIONS

Divide content into 2-4 main sections and write a sentence for each division.

## ESSENCE OF PASSAGE

Write a short sentence (10 words or less!) that gives the thrust of the passage.

## ESSENTIAL QUESTION/AIM

Write the main "transformational truth" to remember from studying this Scripture. Make this as short and simple as possible. It helps to put it in the form of a question to link it to application.

## APPLICATIONS

Write specific questions or challenges to help put the aim into action or answer the question. Are there specific areas in which you need to repent? To believe God and his Word? To live out and apply the gospel?

# Week 9: The Reality of Spiritual Warfare and the Reality of Our Powerful God
## II Corinthians 10

*Realize you're in a war. Prepare a battle plan.*

## GROUP DISCUSSION

✓ *Have you ever felt you were in a spiritual battle? How did you respond?*

## TEACHING TIME

### Know What's Worth Fighting For
### II Corinthians 10-13

- Jesus Christ

- The Gospel

- The Church

- People's Eternal Lives

### Know Where the Battle Is

- In your own minds and hearts

- In your own "community"

- In the world

### Know What/Who the Real Enemy Is

- World

- Flesh

- Devil

### Know How to Fight

- Know your weaknesses

- Know your weapons

- Know your divine power

- Know your divine purpose

## REALITY CHECK

*Do you realize the battle you're in and what divine weapons you have? How are you fighting to submit every thought (idea, motive, desire, decision) to Jesus Christ*

## REAL REALITY: SCRIPTURE MEDITATION

*BELIEVE IT. IT'S TRUE, AND TRUE FOR YOU. AMEN!*

*For though we live in the world, we do not wage war as the world does. The weapons we fight with are not the weapons of the world. On the contrary, they have divine power to demolish strongholds. We demolish arguments and every pretension that sets itself up against the knowledge of God, and we take captive every thought to make it obedient to Christ.  II Corinthians 10:3-5*

# Reality Christianity:
# Radiating Christ in Our Cracked Lives

## Week 9: II Corinthians 10

*The Reality of Spiritual Warfare / The Reality of Our Powerful God*

## The Real War:  Preserving and Advancing the Gospel
## II Corinthians 10-13

In this last section of II Corinthians (chapters 10-13), Paul's tone changes from encouragement and thankfulness as he writes to the repentant majority of believers (chapters 8-9) to a serious warning to the unrepentant minority in the church being influenced by the false apostles. Paul is going to war against rebellion.[73] He shows the reality of spiritual warfare, exposes worldly schemes, and reveals the divine power to pull down the strongholds and take thoughts captive to obedience to Christ (10:3-6). He then defends himself against accusations of his authority and apostleship, the difference in his strongly written letters, his unimpressive appearance and less-impressive rhetorical style (10:7-11). He then takes a deep breath and concedes to play their comparison game, except he focuses on his calling from Christ and his boasting in the Lord alone (10:12-18).

Paul again reveals his heart and desire that their faith will continue to grow and that he and Timothy can continue to expand their ministry to preach the gospel where it has not been heard (10:15-16). The Corinthians were being swayed by super apostles (12:11) who promoted successful, flashy ministry. D. A. Carson states, "The Corinthians were quick to seize every emphasis in Christianity that spoke . . . of spiritual power, of exaltation with Christ, of freedom, triumph, of victorious Christian living. . . but they neglected those accents in Christianity that stressed meekness, servanthood, obedience, humility, and the need to follow Christ in his suffering . . .they understood D-day had arrived but mistook it for V-day. They loved Christian triumphalism, but they did not know how to live under the sign of the cross."[74]

Paul realized that the real battle for the gospel was at stake, the simple, foolish, powerful message of the gospel of the grace of God in Jesus Christ (II Cor. 5:21, Rom. 5:8-11, John 14:6).

## Know What's Worth Fighting For

In Philippians Paul did not attack his preaching "competitors" and, in fact, he rejoiced because whether from false or pure motives, Christ was being preached. (Phil. 1:15-18). In II Corinthians 10-13, he deals

---

73 [1]R. Kent Hughes, *2 Corinthians: Power in Weakness* (Crossway Books: Wheaton, IL, 2006), 180.

74 Hughes, 180.

decisively with the false apostles and those they influenced because they were preaching a different gospel and a different Christ, and they were dividing the church. Paul ends the letter with an appeal to make sure the rebellious Corinthians were really believers (13:5).

He was fighting for Christ, the gospel, the church, and the souls of men and women. Today, many people are swayed by the health and wealth promises for this life by preachers downplaying the reality of sin, the need for personal repentance and exclusive belief in Jesus Christ alone for salvation, the call to embrace the suffering of Christ and his people, to live as ambassadors of reconciliation and to long for our true home in Heaven. Christian and secular bookstores are filled with bestselling titles such as "Your Best Life Now." Paul's warning to the Corinthians applies today.

## Know Where the Battle Is and Who You Are Fighting Against

The battle starts in our minds and hearts. Paul speaks in military terms of strongholds (fortresses, fortified place); arguments (plausible fallacies); lofty opinions (raised ramparts, arrogant attitude, towering conceit, presumptuous notion in defiance of the authentic knowledge of God)[75] When Paul talks about taking captive our thoughts (every idea, motive, desire, decision)[76], it is a picture of "prisoners of war bound hand and foot and turned over to a new authority."[77] Paul is at war with the schemes of Satan attacking our minds. His goal is to take those rebellious thoughts and lead them to Christ. "Paul envisages every rebellious thought or scheme as not only being captured but also being reduced to servitude to Christ or being forced to render allegiance to Christ, the victorious and reigning Lord."[78]

To battle well, you must first be aware you are in a battle, know your weaknesses, know your enemy and his strengths and tactics, and know your weapons and know how to use them. Paul is clearly showing that our struggles often start in our thoughts, minds, and hearts. Our battle is with Satan. He attacks us where we are vulnerable and where we are arrogant. John Piper's approach is to "Give the devil his due but no more."[79] In this very real battle, Piper gives three reminders: 1. Satan can do nothing apart from God's sovereign permission. 2. Jesus dealt the death blow to Satan. Satan can harass us, but he cannot destroy us. 3. Deliverance from Satan's power comes most often from his truth found in Scripture.[80] Paul speaks of our weapons having divine powers. These weapons include Jesus Christ as our righteousness, the Holy Spirit, the Word of God, prayer, our faith (see Eph. 6:10-18), and the body of believers around

---

75 [3] Murray J. Harris, *The Second Epistle to the Corinthians* (Eerdmans Publishing Co: Grand Rapids, MI, 2005), 676-682.

76 *Spirit of the Reformation Study Bible*, Notes on II Cor. 10:5.

77 Harris, 682.

78 Harris, 684.

79 [7] John Piper, *When I Don't Desire God: How to Fight for Joy* (Crossways Books: Wheaton, IL, 2004), 224-225.

80 Piper, 225.

us. Christianity is not a solo sport or guerilla warfare. We are soldiers together, a body, a family which recognizes the battle and fights under the Lordship of Jesus Christ.

## The Battle For Your Minds and Hearts

One of the best weapons as you battle for your thought life is time spent alone with God in prayer and Scripture that flows into time together in community. Henri Nouwen writes of this need for solitude with God, "It's important because it's the place in which you can listen to the voice of the One who calls you the beloved. . . To pray is to let that voice speak to the center of your being, to your guts, and let that voice resound to your whole being. Who am I? I am the beloved."[81] Do you view your time with God in Scripture that way? Do you believe the biggest battle is to believe the truth that you are God's beloved? Not as a way to check off your holy to-do list or get information or a learn a set of rules, but to remember who you really are and who God is and what He has done for you. Nouwen says that's where ministry starts. "When you discover your belovedness by God, you see the belovedness of other people and call that forth. It's an incredible mystery of God's love that the more you know how deeply you are loved, the more you will see how deeply your sisters and brothers in the human family are loved."[82] This opens us up for the beauty of a community of broken, beloved people. "Community is a way of living: you gather around you people with whom you want to proclaim the truth that we are the beloved sons and daughters of God."[83]

Why didn't Paul just give up on the Corinthian church and their false accusations of him and keep heading west to Spain? He knew his identity in Christ, his belovedness, and he longed for these believers to grow in their faith (10:15) and knowledge of their belovedness so they can then share in the grace of the gospel of Jesus Christ and the joy of submitting to his lordship.

---

81  Henri Nouwen, "*Moving from Solitude to Community to Ministry*." Fellowship Bible Church http://www.fbccs.org/resources/papers/soli_comm_mini.asp. Nov. 9, 2009.

82  Ibid.

83  Ibid.

# Week 10: The Reality of Deception
## II Corinthians 11

*Questions marked with an * are for those doing "Bible Study Express."*

**Note on Chapter 11:** *Paul has a passion for the "Real Thing," Jesus Christ and His gospel of grace. He has been teaching about the real Christian life in contrast to the legalistic or deceptive teaching the Corinthians had received. Now Paul has dropped all subtlety in his attack against these false teachers and goes head-to-head and heart-to-heart with them, battling to present the church as a pure virgin for her bridegroom Jesus Christ. We are in the same battle today, in a world filled with flashy presentations, powerful leaders, and false teachings. This week, pray that God would renew your mind (Romans 12:2) so you can discern the truth and know the Real Thing! Be prepared, there are more Scripture references to look up than usual because the Bible is the main tool, along with the Holy Spirit, prayer, and godly counsel, we use to fight deception.*

## Day 1: The Reality of Deceivers

**Read II Corinthians 11:1-15.** What is Paul's main concern and goal for the Corinthians (vs. 2-3)?*

How was Eve deceived in Genesis 3:1-6?

How are we deceived?  See 1 John 2:15-17.*

How does Paul describe the false apostles (vs. 13-15)?*

How do you think they were influencing the Corinthian church?*

In Philippians 1:15-18, Paul allows others to preach Christ out of selfish ambition. In II Corinthians 11, he is opposed to the "super apostles." What is the difference?

Where have you been led astray from your sincere devotion to Christ?*

Where have you allowed yourself to be deceived by style over substance, or because you have not been a Berean (Acts 17:11)?

Ask your group to pray that you will have the desire to know the truth and have undistracted devotion to God. Repent specifically of areas where you have become deceived, distracted, or drawn to different "lovers."*

Consolidate the message of II Corinthians 11 into one sentence. Share that sentence with a family member, friend, or someone in your group this week.

*Optional: Do discovery sheet on II Corinthians 11 found at the end of the weekly lesson.*

**Read II Corinthians 11:1-15.** *In verse 4, what three areas does Paul list as being preached or received differently?**

*Follow the principle of those trained to detect counterfeit bills. They spend all their time studying the real thing. In the same way, focus on the biblical truths about Jesus, the Spirit, and the Gospel and write some essential truths (with biblical references if possible) about them:*

Jesus

Holy Spirit

Gospel

Paul is battling against deception and for truth. What questions do you need to ask to make sure you're not being deceived, especially in a "religious" setting?*

Paul uses the picture of engagement and marriage to describe the relationship of Jesus Christ to the church and speaks of having godly jealousy for them. Read Exodus 20:4-6. As you look at your betrothal and preparation to be a pure bride, is there any idol or other "first love" which would provoke God's jealousy?*

How can you begin to recognize the truth?* Ask God for a renewed passion to study Scripture as a revelation of Himself and His truth.

# Day 3: The Reality of Servant Leadership

 **Read II Corinthians 11:1-15.** From this passage and I Corinthians 2:1-5, what was Paul's leadership style?*

How is that contrasted with the style of the false apostles?*

What are the biblical characteristics of leadership? See John 13:12-17, Titus 1:6-9 and I Timothy 3:1-13.

What are the biblical characteristics of following? See John 10:27-30; Matthew 4:19-20, 16:24-26.

How can a Christian both submit to and have discerning evaluation of their spiritual leaders?*

Why was Paul preaching "free of charge" to the Corinthians, but being supported by the Macedonian believers?

Do you know of a situation where you, a friend, or family member were unduly influenced by false teaching?*

What was the result?*

If it is a current situation, what can you do to loving receive or give the real truth?*

 As you look at Paul's example and the principles of leading and following, how can you be a good leader where you are called to be and how can you be a good follower where you are called to be?*

**Read II Corinthians 11:15-33.** Why did Paul feel like a fool?*

How does he contrast worldly foolishness with his own foolishness?

What was Paul boasting about?* Why do you think he felt compelled to boast?*

In what else has Paul boasted? See II Corinthians 1:12, 9:2, 10:8, 11:10, 11:30 and 12:9. Do these "boastings" contradict his call to boast only in the Lord (II Corinthians 10:17) and the cross of Christ (Galatians 6:14)?

What a picture of Paul as he is lowered in a basket to escape arrest! Where have you had to "lower yourself" or felt helpless and weak even though you were "working for the Lord?"

How can you believe in God's sovereign goodness in your weaknesses? *

 Share with your group a time when you have identified with Paul in being misunderstood or attacked, having to defend yourself, or just feeling like a "fool for Christ."

How did God reveal himself to you in that situation?*

**Read II Corinthians 11:15-33.** What were the Corinthians putting up with (vs. 20)?

List the qualifications and persecutions Paul dares to "boast about."*

After listing all of this, what was Paul's daily pressure (vs. 28-29)?*

What pressures, concerns, and weaknesses are you dealing with now?

Share with your group how they can pray for you in one (or more) of these areas.*

 How concerned are you for those within your church family who are weak or are led into sin? Think of specific ways you can pray and come alongside family or church members and show them your love and concern.*

# OPTIONAL PERSONAL DISCOVERY SHEET

II Corinthians 11

## CONTENT

List the main points from this Scripture.

## DIVISIONS

Divide content into 2-4 main sections and write a sentence for each division.

## ESSENCE OF PASSAGE

Write a short sentence (10 words or less!) that gives the thrust of the passage.

## ESSENTIAL QUESTION/AIM

Write the main "transformational truth" to remember from studying this Scripture. Make this as short and simple as possible. It helps to put it in the form of a question to link it to application.

## APPLICATIONS

Write specific questions or challenges to help put the aim into action or answer the question. Are there specific areas in which you need to repent? To believe God and his Word? To live out and apply the gospel?

# Week 10: The Reality of Deception
## II Corinthians 11

## GROUP DISCUSSION

✓ *How do you learn to discern the "Real Thing?"*

## TEACHING TIME

BACKGROUND OF II CORINTHIANS 11:

PAUL'S FEARS: (vs. 4, 20, 28-29)

PAUL'S FOCUS: (vs. 1-3, 12, 30)

PAUL'S GOAL: (vs. 3)

### KNOW AND ACCEPT THE REAL YOU

Descendants of Adam and Eve (vs. 3-4)

*Live the mystery of "both-and." You are **both** an easily distracted, comparison-shopping, pain-avoiding sin addict **and** a chosen, beloved son and daughter of the King redeemed by Jesus Christ.*

### KNOW AND LOVE THE REAL THING
### II Corinthians 11

#### THE REAL JESUS
HIS BEING: Fully God, fully man, Messiah, Lord, Savior.

HIS CLAIM: The one and only way to God and heaven.

HIS WORK: Complete, sufficient, finished.
*John 1:1-14, 3:36, 14:6, 19:30, 20:31; Matt. 16:13-17; I Cor. 15:14-28, II Co.r 5:21, Co.l 1:15-20; I John 4:9-10.*

## THE REAL SPIRIT

HIS BEING: One with Father and Son, fully God

HIS WORK: Indweller, Guarantee, Assurance, Power, Interceder, Comforter, Connecter, Helper, Transformer

HIS FRUIT: Freedom, love, joy, peace, power

*II Cor. 1:21-22, 3:17, Rom. 8:15-16, 14:17-18, 15:13; Gal. 5:1, 22; 2 Tim. 1:7; I Cor. 2:12*

## THE REAL GOSPEL

Just Jesus. Jesus + anything else is not the Gospel.

We are saved from our sins and reconciled to God through the life, death, resurrection of Jesus Christ. Repent and believe and be saved.

*Jn. 3:16, Eph. 2:8-9, Gal. 1:6-9, 2:4-5, Rom. 3:23-24, 5:1-11, 6:23, 10:9-13*

## THE REAL MINISTER/MINISTRY/CHURCH

## LEARN TO DISCERN THE REAL THING
## II Corinthians 11

✓ Know your weaknesses. Know your strength (in Christ).

✓ Read Scripture and learn to think biblically.

✓ Know and share the simple truth.

✓ Be a Berean. (Acts 17:11)

✓ Be accountable and a member of Bible-believing church.

✓ Pray individually and corporately.

✓ Examine fruit/lifestyle.

✓ Be aware of the schemes of Satan:

> *Distract from devotion*
> *Doubt God's word*
> *Deceive*
> *Depress*
> *Dominate*

- ✓ Be aware of false prophets' methods:
    - *Enslave*
    - *Exploit*
    - *Exalt self instead of Christ*
    - *Put others down*

- ✓ Questions to ask:

    - *Is this consistent with Scripture?*
    - *Is this focused on exalting and giving an accurate portrayal of the Lord Jesus Christ?*
    - *Is this person's lifestyle (walk, fruit) consistent with Bible?*

## REALITY CHECK

Is Jesus Christ your first love and focus of life? If not, what or whom is taking His place? How has your devotion to Christ changed you and impacted those around you?

## REAL REALITY: SCRIPTURE MEDITATION

*BELIEVE IT. IT'S TRUE, AND TRUE FOR YOU. AMEN!*

*But I am afraid that just as Eve was deceived by the serpent's cunning, your minds may somehow be led astray from your sincere and pure devotion to Christ. II Cor. 11:3*

*Besides everything else, I face daily the pressure of my concern for all the churches. Who is weak, and I do not feel weak? Who is led into sin, and I do not inwardly burn? II Corinthians 11:28-29*

# The Apostles' Creed

I believe in God, the Father almighty,
    creator of heaven and earth.

I believe in Jesus Christ, his only Son, our Lord.
    He was conceived by the power of the Holy Spirit
        and born of the Virgin Mary.

    He suffered under Pontius Pilate,
    was crucified, died, and was buried.

    He descended to the dead.

    On the third day he rose again.

    He ascended into heaven,
        and is seated at the right hand of the Father.

    He will come again to judge the living and the dead.

I believe in the Holy Spirit,
    the holy catholic Church,
    the communion of saints,
    the forgiveness of sins,
    the resurrection of the body,
    and the life everlasting.  Amen.

# The Nicene Creed

We believe in one God,
    the Father, the Almighty,
    maker of heaven and earth,
    of all that is, seen and unseen.

We believe in one Lord, Jesus Christ,
    the only Son of God,
    eternally begotten of the Father,
    God from God, Light from Light,
    true God from true God,
    begotten, not made,
    of one Being with the Father.
    Through him all things were made.
For us and for our salvation
    he came down from heaven:
by the power of the Holy Spirit
    he became incarnate from the Virgin Mary,
    and was made man.
For our sake he was crucified under Pontius
Pilate;
    he suffered death and was buried.
    On the third day he rose again
      in accordance with the Scriptures;
    he ascended into heaven
    and is seated at the right hand of the Father.
He will come again in glory to judge the living
and the dead,
    and his kingdom will have no end.

We believe in the Holy Spirit, the Lord, the giver
of life,
    who proceeds from the Father and the Son.
    With the Father and the Son he is worshiped
    and glorified.
    He has spoken through the Prophets.
    We believe in one holy catholic and apostolic
    Church.
    We acknowledge one baptism for the forgiveness
    of sins.
    We look for the resurrection of the dead,
      and the life of the world to come. Amen.

# Reality Christianity:
# Radiating Christ in Our Cracked Lives

## Week 10: II Corinthians 11

*The Reality of Deception / The Reality of Our True God*

## Father of the Bride:  Paul Goes to Battle for Christ's Bride

Paul knows what to fight for: the real Jesus, the real Spirit, the real gospel, and the Bride of Christ (the Church). In II Cor. 11, Paul takes the gloves off against the pseudo, "super" apostles who are taking the Bride's eyes off Jesus Christ, her Bridegroom. Paul sees himself in the role of the matchmaker or father with a divine jealousy to present a sincere, pure, and devoted bride (11:3) to the Bridegroom. "Paul is alarmed that the bride-to-be is flirting with a Jesus other than the Jesus we preach (11:4) and is dangerously close to being unfaithful to the true Jesus . . . a sincere devotion to Christ is possible only where the true and authentic gospel of Christ is taught and heard (11:3). Christians need to think about *what* they are being taught rather than being impressed by *who* is teaching them, however winsome he or she may be."[84] The Corinthians were facing a choice, that ultimately Eve faced in the Garden of Eden. Would they believe God, or would they be lured by Satan's deceptive promises? "The betrothed Corinthian community . . . were susceptible to Satan's cunning as he led them away from Christ into the promise of a more triumphant, victorious, prosperous Christianity—a Christianity that was dismissive of taking up the cross and weakness and suffering. . .the wolves in the church that devour sheep do not howl and bare their teeth. They come in sheep's clothing, smiling, reciting Scripture, full of understanding, promising something more than Jesus."[85]

Paul is battling a mix of two cultures. First, he was up against the Greek culture that valued appearances, rhetorical style, power, money, position and boasting. Because they didn't believe in the afterlife, everyone was fighting for glory and honor in this life. Second, Paul was battling the Judaizers, who kept trying to re-insert the law, circumcision, rituals, and old Covenant into the simplicity of the gospel. Paul battled not with the same rhetorical 'techniques,' but with true knowledge of God (11:6), with a heart for the real Jesus, Spirit, and gospel (11:4) and a bleeding pastoral heart for the believers (11:28-29) in their struggle against sin and weakness. His battle is with Satan, who cunningly disguises himself as an angel of light (11:14). "When Satan is at work, we never smell sulfur or glance down at a cloven hoof; rather he

---

84 [1] Paul Barnett, *The Message of 2 Corinthians* (Inter-Varsity Press:  Downers Grove, IL, 1988), 164.

85 [2] R. Kent Hughes, *2 Corinthians: Power in Weakness* (Crossway Books: Wheaton, IL, 2006), 176.

is sweetness and a congenial, smiling light—until he has control."[86] His first technique is to lure us into to thinking he doesn't exist or isn't relevant today. In a scene from the television series, *Criminal Minds*, the logical (and secular) agent was explaining to another agent who doubted the existence of a satanic power, "If you believe in one, you have to believe in the other." Awareness of the reality of the battle is the first step. The second step is awareness of who you are.

## Know and Accept the Real You vs. "Super-You"

Paul knows the reality of who we are: the daughters of Eve and sons of Adam. We are easily deceived, and our minds are easily distracted (11:3) by our own flesh, by the attraction of the world, and the wiles of Satan (see Gen. 3:1-7). We must begin by accepting the mystery that we are *"both-and."* We are *both* easily distracted, comparison-shopping, pain avoiding sin addicts *and* chosen, beloved, redeemed royal sons and daughters of the King and the beautiful bride of Jesus Christ. Paul shows us a contrast on who we will follow: the flashy, self-promoting, highly paid presenter; or the simple truth giver whose credentials includes much suffering, persecution, pressure, and weakness. Often, we follow what we want to become. It's difficult to not choose the pain-free "package." We want to look and sound as good as the super apostles. We fear the reality of where being a minister of the gospel will lead. The mystic Teresa of Avila said tongue-in-cheek of God, "If this is the way you treat your friends, it's no wonder you have so few!"

## Know and Love the Real Jesus, Spirit, Gospel

Paul lists the three areas of deep concern he has for the Corinthians. They were being led away by a different Jesus, different Spirit, and different gospel. Would you be able to discern the real thing? We must become like those who can detect counterfeit bills. They train by studying the real bills so that when they see a fake, they know something is wrong.

Study the Bible in context if you want to know the real Christ, the real Spirit, and the real gospel. Review the basic catechisms (Westminster and Heidelberg) and creeds (Apostles and Nicene) which are rooted in Scripture. Through history, these have stood the tests of synods and critics to present the undeniable essential truths of Christianity. Please refer to this lesson's handout to check out Scriptures on Jesus, the Spirit, and the gospel your own. Meditate on the essential truths found in the Apostles' and Nicene Creed.

## Learn to Discern the Real Thing

We must learn to discern the real thing because we live in an environment where political, church, and business leaders can easily manipulate Christians for personal gain or power. We've become a "spell-

---

86 Hughes, 199.

check" generation, confident others are looking out for errors. We should become like the Bereans (Acts 17:11) who go back to Scriptures to verify what has been said is true. We should examine the lifestyle and "fruit" of those who desire to exercise influence over us and look for the warning flags Paul highlights about the super apostles: they enslave, exploit, exalt themselves and look down on their followers (11:20). Finally, be aware of Satan's schemes to distract, divide, and deceive. From II Corinthians, Paul shows three of Satan's methods: "First, Satan seeks to divide and weaken the body of Christ by bitterness and unforgiveness (2:10-11). Second, Satan seeks to maintain sinners in their spiritual blindness, unable to see the glory of Christ (4:4). Third, Satan, above all else, seeks to sever the believer from Christ by means of false doctrine about Christ (11:3, 14).[87]

## Paul's Foolish "Boastings"

As Paul recalled the humiliation of lowering himself in a basket (11:33), he now lowers himself to the level of the false apostles by playing their own game of boasting. But he does it with a godly twist. He begins with his pedigree: He one-upped them all (11:22) in his ethnic (Hebrew), religious (Israelite), and covenantal (Abraham) heritage.[88] He then figuratively pulls his shirt off to show that his scars and suffering, not success and oratory skills, validate his ministry. After the list of physical sufferings, he revealed his greatest pain was for his people (11:28-29), for their pain and their struggle with sin. He concludes with a boast of his weakness. "Weakness is the singular apostolic qualification, not human strength. This, too, flies in the face of today's resume-obsessed culture which worships strength and beauty and intelligence and pedigree and success."[89] Are you willing to let God, not culture, write your Christian "resume" for His glory?

---

87 Barnett, 170.

88 Hughes 202.

89 Hughes, 206-7.

# Week 11: The Reality of Weakness
## II Corinthians 12:1-10

*Questions marked with an * are for those doing "Bible Study Express."*

## Day 1: God's Revelation to Paul

 **Read II Corinthians 12:1-10.** Why is Paul reluctant to talk about his visions and revelations (verses 3-6)?

So, why did he bring it up?*

What does Paul mean by the third heaven or paradise (See Gen. 2, Heb. 4:14, 7:26, Eph. 4:10, Rev. 2:7.)

 Have you, like Paul, had a special experience or revelation from God?

How can it be a reminder of God's love and purpose for your life without it becoming your defining spiritual moment? Or, in other words, how do you balance your past spiritual experiences with your present walk and future hope in God?*

*"I coulda' been a contender."* As you grow older, do you sometimes wish that people knew who you were or what you did in the past for God? Are you willing to trust God in what might be a less dramatic ministry or less visible season of your life?

 Paul's main concern in verse 6 was refraining from speaking too much about his special revelations so *"no one will think more of me than is warranted by what I do or say."* How do you want people to see you?

Are you willing to let them see your weaknesses?

Do you want them to think "more of you?" Or do you want them to think more of Jesus?*

Consolidate the message of II Corinthians 12:1-10 into one sentence. Share that sentence with a family member, friend, or someone in your group this week.

*Optional: Do discovery sheet on II Corinthians 12:1-10 found at the end of the weekly lesson.*

## Day 2: Paul's Plea to God

 **Read II Corinthians 12:1-10.** What did Paul want? What did he get? Did he get what he needed?*

What could Paul's "thorn in the flesh" have been? (See also Acts 9:9, Gal. 4:15, 6:11, II Cor. 7:5.)

Why do you think it's not specifically named?

What good could have been accomplished by Paul's thorn?

Who gave Paul this thorn (verse 7)?*

How does Paul view God's part and Satan's part in his thorn?

When your prayers seem to go unanswered or are denied, how do you view God?

How do you live in the tension of desire and disappointment, and of trusting and waiting?

 How will you believe God is good and good to you instead of despairing that God is "holding out on you" if your thorn is not removed?*

Think and pray through an unresolved "thorn" in your life and how you view God's part and Satan's part in this difficulty. Write an honest prayer to God with repentance and belief (and ask for help for your unbelief) about this issue.*

**Read II Corinthians 12:1-10.** God's answer to Paul's cry for help and release:

*My grace is sufficient for you, for my power is made perfect in weakness.*

Meditate on this verse and define each of these words (using a dictionary, synonym guide, or Bible dictionary). Put other Biblical references which may help you more fully understand God's answer to Paul:*

Paul:*

Grace

Sufficient

Power

Made Perfect

Weakness

Where have you pleaded with God?

Where have you experienced God's sufficient grace? God's power?*

 What can you do to develop trust in God during times of weakness and what seems like unanswered prayers?*

**Read II Corinthians 12:1-10.** Write down in your own words Paul's response to God's answer (verses 9-10) to his thorn.*

List what Paul delighted in from verse 10. Why did he delight in these undelightful things?*

How does Paul's life live out his statement *"When I am weak, then I am strong"*?

Paul talks of Christ's power 'resting' on him. Read Isaiah 30:15-18 and Matthew 11:28-30. What is God's desire?

What does man's flesh tend to do?

How do II Corinthians 11:30 and 12:10 reflect the theme of the entire letter to the Corinthians?*

Write down one way God has worked through your weakness in a way that He has been glorified and you have been given sufficient grace and power.*

Do you want to be delivered *from* or have God's power *in* your thorn or weakness? Why?

 Re-read II Corinthians 12:10 and be honest before God. Have you ever delighted in weaknesses, in insults, in hardships, in persecution, in difficulties?

Share a time when you could sense that the hardship you were experiencing seemed to either glorify God or help you identify with Christ.*

**Read II Corinthians 12:1-10.** Rewrite II Corinthians 12:7-10 in your own words as if you were writing it to someone unfamiliar with Christianity or this passage.*

Give an example of the "weak/strong" paradox (verse 10) from your own life or someone else's.

Who gives you more hope, those who have it all together or those who have struggled, but have experienced God's grace and power? Why?

Do you always try to fix your weaknesses?

Where do you need to trust God's power and grace in your life and let go of self-effort?*

What have you learned from the ongoing struggles or unremoved thorns in your life?*

How can you distinguish between a God-glorifying thorn in your life and when you're the "thorn" in someone else's life?

 Think of people who have made an impact on your life. How have their struggles encouraged you?*

# OPTIONAL PERSONAL DISCOVERY SHEET

II Corinthians 12:1-10

## CONTENT

List the main points from this Scripture.

## DIVISIONS

Divide content into 2-4 main sections and write a sentence for each division.

## ESSENCE OF PASSAGE

Write a short sentence (10 words or less!) that gives the thrust of the passage.

## ESSENTIAL QUESTION/AIM

Write the main "transformational truth" to remember from studying this Scripture. Make this as short and simple as possible. It helps to put it in the form of a question to link it to application.

## APPLICATIONS

Write specific questions or challenges to help put the aim into action or answer the question. Are there specific areas in which you need to repent? To believe God and his Word? To live out and apply the gospel?

# Week 11: The Reality of Weakness
## II Corinthians 12:1-10

## GROUP DISCUSSION

✓ *How have you experienced Christ's sufficient grace and power in your weaknesses? Have you been able to accept your weaknesses?*

## TEACHING TIME

*"Ah, if you knew what power there is in an accepted sorrow."*
*Madame Guyon*

### PAUL'S REVELATIONS/YOUR REVELATIONS
### II Corinthians 12:1-6

Background:

Third heaven:

Paul's revelations:

Your revelations:

### PAUL REALITIES/YOUR REALITIES
### II Corinthians 12:7-8

Paul's reality:

Your reality:

## CHRIST'S RESPONSE/YOUR RESPONSE
## II Corinthians 12:9-10

Christ's Response:

*My grace is sufficient for you for my power is made perfect in weakness.*

Paul's Response:

*Once I heard that, I was glad to let it happen. I quit focusing on the handicap and began appreciating the gift. It was a case of Christ's strength moving in on my weakness. Now I take limitations in stride, and with good cheer, these limitations that cut me down to size—abuse, accidents, opposition, bad breaks. I just let Christ take over! And so the weaker I get, the stronger I become. II Cor. 12:9-10 The Message*

Your Response:

# REALITY CHECK

Where are you denying your weakness and where do you need to release and receive God's grace, strength, and power?

# REAL REALITY: SCRIPTURE MEDITATION

*BELIEVE IT. IT'S TRUE, AND TRUE FOR YOU. AMEN!*

*But he said to me, "My grace is sufficient for you, for my power is made perfect in weakness." Therefore, I will boast all the more gladly about my weaknesses, so that Christ's power may rest on me. That is why, for Christ's sake, I delight in weaknesses, in insults, in hardships, in persecutions, in difficulties. For when I am weak, then I am strong. II Corinthians 12:9-10*

# Reality Christianity:
# Radiating Christ in Our Cracked Lives
## Week 11: II Corinthians 12:1-10
*The Reality of Weakness / The Reality of Our Sufficient God*

## Paul Reveals "Reality Christianity"
## II Corinthians 12:1-10

In II Corinthians 10-13, Paul takes the gloves off to defend real Christ-glorifying ministry in contrast to the super apostles' self-focused influence on the Corinthians with their boastings, visions, rhetorical skills, physical appearances, promises, and "successful" ministry model. They've drawn Paul into a battle he hates (going head-to-head comparing pedigree, visions, calling, authority) but he turns it upside down in these ten verses and gives the whole theme of this book and ringing truth of reality Christianity. We do not "do" ministry out of our strengths, talents, visions, successes. Christ ministers to others through our weaknesses. He is sufficient. He will give the power and grace needed. He will get the glory.

"The grand theme, the melodic line, of 2 Corinthians is authentic ministry . . . and the persistent motif of authentic ministry is *power in weakness*. . . . Paul's utter weakness was the platform for resurrection power. . .'Power in weakness' runs as a thread throughout the letter, reaching its most powerful expression here."[90] The thread runs from Paul's opening statement of utter despair even of life and reliance on the God who raises the dead (1:8-9); to his word picture of God's surpassing power in cracked clay pots (4:7-12); and the paradox of poor-yet-rich, dying-yet-bringing-life ministry (6:4-10) culminating in Christ's words to Paul, "My grace is sufficient for you, for my power is made perfect in weakness." (12:9)

## Paul's Private Revelations Made Public
## II Corinthians 12:1-6

Paul's use of the third person (*I know a man* vs. 2) shows his hesitancy to share his intimate revelations from God because it was not the basis of his ministry or his identity. This revelation occurred 14 years prior (42-44 AD) when Paul was in Tarsus or Antioch, before he began his missionary journeys. It possibly was one way God prepared him for his ministry. Paul describes it as he was caught up to the *third heaven* and *paradise*. "This phrase (third heaven) does not imply belief in a simplistic 'three-story' universe' but reflects a common sense distinction between (1) the atmosphere where birds can be seen

---

90 [1]R. Kent Hughes, *2 Corinthians: Power in Weakness* (Crossway Books: Wheaton, IL, 2006), 213-4.

to fly, (2) the higher area where the sun, moon, and stars can be seen, and (3) the unseen realm where God dwells. This third area is equated with paradise (Gk. *paradeisos*, a Persian loan-word used in the Septuagint to refer to the Garden of Eden but in the New Testament to refer to a place of blessedness where God dwells (Luke 23:43, Rev. 2:7)."[91]

Paul relished Christ, not the 'rare moment' of revelation. Many people live for the dramatic 'mountaintop' moment and are shocked by the ordinariness and hard work of 'in-the-valley' ministry. "If you make a god of your best moments, you will find that God will fade out of your life and never come back until you do the duty that lies nearest and have learned not to make a fetish of your rare moments."[92]

What about you? Are you waiting for God to keep giving you special revelations and experiences when you have his Word and Spirit to do the next right thing? For Paul, his 'thorn' popped any bubble he may have had about how special he was because of the vision he received.

Do you want people to think more of you or of Christ (12:6)? Do you want others to see you as special or Christ as powerful and gracious in your struggles and weaknesses? Paul is saying to the Corinthians: "I want you to look at what I am, not what I was. The man I want you to take into account is not the one who experienced an astonishing revelation then but the one you see now, in all his weakness."[93]

## Paul's Realities and Request
## II Corinthians 12:7-8

If you have been thinking of Paul as an out-of-reach super saint, he reveals himself in vs. 7-8 in all his humanity and vulnerability. He shows his struggle and what could be seen as failure to get his prayers answered. Paul begs God to remove his thorn (Gr. *skolops*) three times. In the Greek this means *stake* (pinning him down) or *splinter* (constant irritant and reminder). "The effect of its presence was to cripple Paul's enjoyment of life and to frustrate his full efficiency by draining his energies."[94] Eugene Peterson in *The Message* paraphrases Paul's struggle (12:7-9), "Because of the extravagance of those revelations, and so I wouldn't get a big head, I was given the gift of a handicap to keep me in constant touch with my limitations. Satan's angel did his best to get me down; what he in fact did was push me to my knees. No danger then of walking around high and mighty! At first, I didn't think of it as a gift, and begged God to remove it. Three times I did that, and then he told me, My grace is enough; it's all you need. My strength comes into its own in your weakness."

---

91 *ESV Study Bible*, Notes on II Corinthians 12:2-3.

92 Oswald Chambers, *My Utmost for His Highest*, 4/25 entry.

93 Paul Barnett, *The Message of 2 Corinthians* (Inter-Varsity Press: Downers Grove, IL, 1988), 177.

94 Barnett, 177.

**Who gave this thorn to Paul?** "While the thorn was Satan's work, it was God who allowed it."[95]

**What was this thorn or handicap?** Paul does not specify. This is a comfort to all of us who have thorns of our own. We can identify with the struggle and not dismiss our own thorns as less significant. Commentators have speculated that Paul's thorn could have been *spiritual or psychological* (depression, guilt over his former persecution of Christians, concern over Israel's unbelief, Satan's attack); personal *opposition* to Paul by an individual or group such as the false apostles; or *physical* (malarial fever, poor eyesight, migraines).[96] What is known about the thorn is that it was a consequence of his revelation, caused him constant pain, was permanent, humbling, humiliating, and made Paul feel weak.[97] Most commentators lean toward a physical 'thorn.'

Paul prayed three times similar to Jesus Christ's thrice-repeated prayer (Mk. 14:32-41) in the Garden of Gethsemane. Like Jesus, he did not see this prayer as his failure (if only I had prayed more fervently, or God had loved me more) or God's failure. He submitted to God's will. "The messengers of Satan are not always overthrown here and now by prevailing prayer, though they will be overthrown ultimately; neither is it necessarily the will of God that his children 'triumph' in this life in terms of body healing or spiritual power. The 'thorn' from God kept Paul from imagining himself as a spiritual superman and revealed to him the reality of his human mortality and weakness despite his extraordinary revelations. The 'thorn' also kept Paul pinned close to the Lord, in trust and confidence."[98]

Oh, beloved of God, struggling with your own thorn, will it make you turn inward or turn upward? Madame Guyon states, "Ah, if you knew what power there is in an accepted sorrow." In the same way, do you know the power in accepted weakness?

## God's Response
## II Corinthians 12:9

If you have a "red-letter" Bible, God's response to Paul's (12:9) repeated prayer pops out at you. "My grace is sufficient for you, for my power is made perfect in weakness." Dwell on each word:

*My/you*: A personal God directly answers Paul.

*Grace*: Gift, kindness, unmerited favor, mercy, powerful intervention.

---

95 Hughes, 212.

96 Murray J. Harris, *The Second Epistle to the Corinthians* (Eerdmans Publishing Co: Grand Rapids, MI, 2005), 858.

97 Harris, 857.

98 Barnett, 178.

*Is:* Perfect tense, timeless 'durative' present. "For Paul, his urgent requests were a memory of the past, but Christ's reassuring answer was a reality of the present."[99] Right now, and for the duration, Christ's grace and power are yours in your ongoing weaknesses.

*Sufficient:* Enough, adequate, plenty, ample, satisfactory.

*For you:* Again, you must see this as an amazing personal God-to-you answer and gift.

*Power:* authority, strength, might, energy, vigor, ability, capacity, capability (from Gr. *dynamo*).

*Perfect:* Ideal, faultless, complete, unspoiled, absolute, whole, finished, total.

*Weakness:* flaw, frailty, feebleness, debility, handicap, infirmity, powerlessness, vulnerability, defenselessness, helplessness, limitation, failing, drawback, difficulty.

"**Power in weakness is shorthand for the cross of Christ.** In God's plan of redemption, there had to be weakness (crucifixion) before there was power (resurrection). And this power-in-weakness connection is what Paul reflected on when he contemplated Christ's praying three times amidst his weakness and powerlessness in Gethsemane before his death on a cross, which was followed by the power of his resurrection."[100]

## Paul's Response to God's Response
## II Corinthians 12:9-10

Paul's response to God's response is "*Therefore I will boast all the more gladly of my weaknesses, so that the power of Christ may rest upon me. For the sake of Christ, then, I am content with weaknesses, insults, hardships, persecutions, and calamities. For when I am weak, then I am strong.*" (II Cor. 12:9-10)

"Paul came to understand and embrace the fact that his thorn in the flesh was essential to his ongoing weakness and the experience of Christ's ongoing power."[101] This is the essence of reality Christianity. We experience the paradox of God's power and grace in our ongoing weakness. "The greatest blessing spiritually is the knowledge that we are destitute . . . He can do nothing for us if we think we are sufficient of ourselves; we have to enter into His Kingdom through the door of destitution."[102]

---

99  Harris, 862.

100  Hughes, 214.

101  Hughes, 214.

102  Oswald Chambers, *My Utmost for His Highest*, 11/28 entry.

When Paul speaks of the power of Christ resting on him, he is painting a beautiful tabernacle image (Exod. 40:34) of Christ dwelling or pitching his tent among his needy people (John 1:14).[103] Can you be still enough—even in your pain—to allow Christ's power to rest on you? Read Matthew 11:28-30 and Isaiah 30:15-18 and meditate on resting in Christ's power. How will you respond? Will you meditate on the cross and resurrection as the ultimate paradox and victory of power in weakness for your redemption? Will you ask boldly for release of the thorn? And if the answer is not yet, will you, for Christ's sake, be content with the realities of this fallen life? The alternative is a bitter, self-pitying life which views God as powerless, uncaring, or cruelly holding out. "In some mysterious way it is within God's plan that our present existence is marked by sin and suffering. From one point of view God abhors and hates these things and will one day overthrow them. And yet is it not through the awareness of our sins that the grace of God holds us near Christ for forgiveness right through our lives? And is it not, also, in the pain of suffering of both body and mind, that the same grace pins us closer to Christ, who says to us, 'My power is made perfect in weakness'?"[104]

Be still and allow Christ's grace and power to rest on you.

---

103 Hughes, 215.

104 Barnett, 180.

# Week 12: The Reality of REALigion
## II Corinthians 12:11-13:14

*Questions marked with an * are for those doing "Bible Study Express."*

## Day 1: Paul's Real Concern for the Corinthians

**Read II Corinthians 12:11-13:14.** Paul wraps up his letter with his concerns for his "children" being swayed by "super-apostles." What were some ways these super-apostles attacked Paul and tried to deceive the Corinthians about his ministry? (See also II Cor. 2:7, 10:8-10, 11:5-7)

What are the signs of a true apostle?*

What is Paul's real concern and fears for the Corinthians (II Cor. 12:19-21, 13:5-10)?*

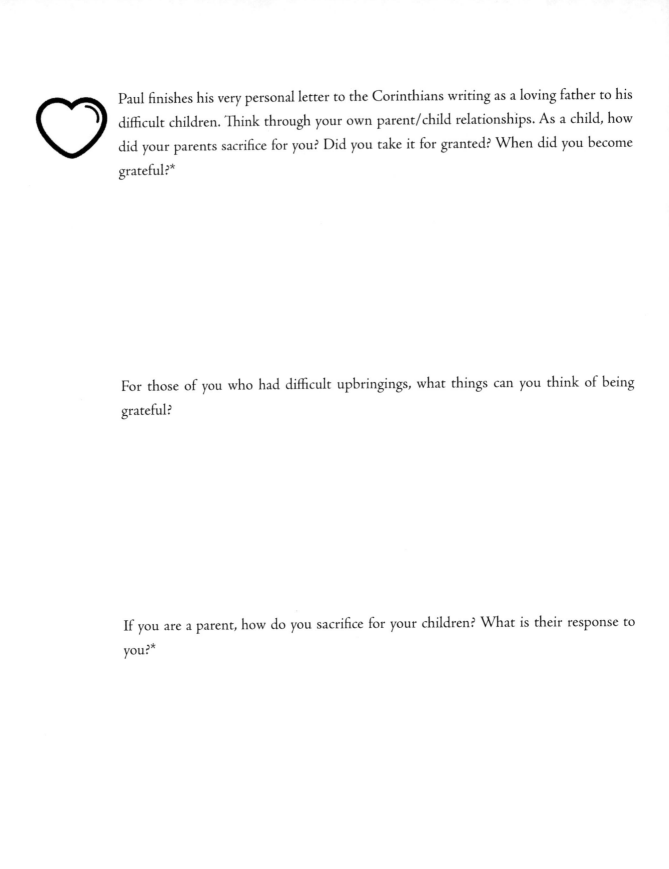

Paul finishes his very personal letter to the Corinthians writing as a loving father to his difficult children. Think through your own parent/child relationships. As a child, how did your parents sacrifice for you? Did you take it for granted? When did you become grateful?*

For those of you who had difficult upbringings, what things can you think of being grateful?

If you are a parent, how do you sacrifice for your children? What is their response to you?*

Think about Paul's "being spent" for those he ministered to. To whom is God leading you to minister to? How will it cost you?*

Spend time writing a letter of thanks to your parents for what they sacrificed for you. (For those of you whose parents have died, it can still be a special experience. For those of you who have difficult relationships with your parents, pray and ask God for understanding into their lives and for some special memory he can bring forth.)

Consolidate the message of II Corinthians 12:11-13:14 into one sentence. Share that sentence with a family member, friend, or someone in your group this week.

*Optional: Do discovery sheet on II Corinthians 12:11-13:14 found at the end of the weekly lesson.*

**Read II Corinthians 12:11-13:14.** Describe Paul's heart for the Corinthians (see 12:19, 13:9-10).*

Paul lovingly, passionately confronts sin. How had the Corinthian church responded in the past?

How do you think you would have received his admonitions?

Are you grieved over other people's sins for Christ's and their own spiritual sake or just how it affects you or your family?

How can you show passionate concern for another's spiritual life without falling into gossip or arrogance?*

 Paul fears that there will be quarreling, jealousy, outbursts of anger, factions, slander, gossip, arrogance, and disorder when he comes to visit the Corinthian church. Think over your past week in your home, work, or church life. Which of these sins are you struggling with?

Be brave! Ask your group to pray that God will reveal your sin and transform you through Christ.*

**Read II Corinthians 13:1-14.** The Corinthians had challenged Paul's credentials. What is Paul's challenge to the Corinthians?*

How can someone test herself to see if she is in the faith?*

What was Paul's prayer and longing for the Corinthian believers? (See Col. 1:9-13, Eph. 1:15-19, 3:14-21 to experience Paul's heart and prayers for believers.)

How do you pray for other believers?

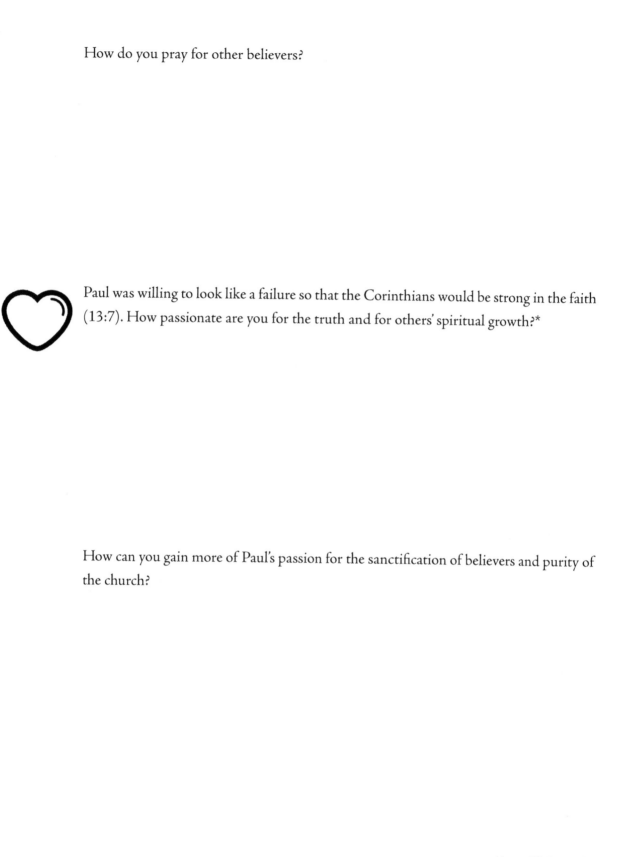

Paul was willing to look like a failure so that the Corinthians would be strong in the faith (13:7). How passionate are you for the truth and for others' spiritual growth?*

How can you gain more of Paul's passion for the sanctification of believers and purity of the church?

Knowing Paul's concern and passions, how would you prepare for Paul's visit to your home or church?

Write down specific areas that you desire God to transform in your life so you can have a life of pure and sincere devotion to Christ.*

**Read II Corinthians 13:1-14.** The questions for this day are extremely important. Take your time and pray through each question and the Scriptures. Don't rush through these. Think of this as your "big test."

What does it mean to be in Christ? See also Colossians 1:27, Ephesians 1:1-14, Romans 6:1-11, and John 15:5-8 for more insight.

How can someone know they are a Christian? List biblical references to support your answer.*

How can you live by faith and assurance of who you really are (if you are in the faith and in Christ)?*

Are you building others up or tearing them down? Examine your words, attitudes, facial expressions, thought life, and heart.

How can you specifically build up those closest to you this week?*

 Examine yourself. Are you in Christ? How do you know? If you are not sure, you can be sure. Please speak to one of your pastors, teachers, small group leaders, or godly friends. Read John 20:31 and Romans 10:9-13.*

**Read II Corinthians 13:11-14.** What is Paul's main desire for the Corinthians in his parting words?*

Paul exalts the Triune God in this benediction. Give the attributes of each Person of the Trinity found in these verses:

GOD

JESUS

SPIRIT

How can you aim for perfection and be content in weakness at the same time?*

The Trinity is almost inconceivable to our finite minds. Which of the Three Persons do you desire to know more about and experience more of? How can you better know and worship the Triune God?*

Write a benediction focused on those you are ministering to (family, friends, church, outreach, etc.). Include worship and praise to our Triune God and your heart's desire for the lives of those you are writing to. Pray it and share it with them.*

# OPTIONAL PERSONAL DISCOVERY SHEET

II Corinthians 12:11-13:14

## CONTENT

List the main points from this Scripture.

## DIVISIONS

Divide content into 2-4 main sections and write a sentence for each division.

## ESSENCE OF PASSAGE

Write a short sentence (10 words or less!) that gives the thrust of the passage.

## ESSENTIAL QUESTION/AIM

Write the main "transformational truth" to remember from studying this Scripture. Make this as short and simple as possible. It helps to put it in the form of a question to link it to application.

## APPLICATIONS

Write specific questions or challenges to help put the aim into action or answer the question. Are there specific areas in which you need to repent? To believe God and his Word? To live out and apply the gospel?

# Week 12 REALigion
## II Corinthians 12:11-13:14

---

## GROUP DISCUSSION

✓ *"Reality"Checks: What do you most desire for and from those you walk with spiritually? How do you know that you are a Christian?*

### TEST PAUL:  THE SPIRITUAL PARENT
### II Corinthians 12:11-13:14

*The True Marks of Paul's Ministry:*

| | |
|---|---|
| Changed lives: | II Cor. 3:2-3 |
| Character of minister, ministry: | II Cor. 6:3-10, 7:2, 8:20-21 |
| Genuine love for church: | II Cor. 6:11-12, 7:3, 11:7-11 |
| Endurance of suffering: | II Cor. 6:3-10, 11:23-33 |
| Signs, wonders, miracles: | II Cor. 12:12 |

*The True Heart of Paul's Ministry from II Cor. 12:11-13:14*

✓ I seek not what is yours but you.

✓ I will most gladly spend and be spent for your souls.

✓ Everything I do is for your strengthening and building up.

✓ I will remind you that you are beloved by the Lord and me.

✓ I will keep loving you even when criticized and falsely accused.

- ✓ I will fear for you and grieve over your sin.

- ✓ I will speak truth and not spare those who are unrepentant in sin.

- ✓ I will challenge you to see if you are in Christ.

- ✓ I will live with Christ to serve you by the power of God.

- ✓ I'm glad when I am weak or seem to fail if you're strong and pass the test.

- ✓ My prayer is for your restoration.

- ✓ I will come in the authority the Lord gave me for building you up, not tearing you down.

*Reality Check #1: Your True Heart for Ministry*

Look at the list above. Do you so desire others' spiritual growth, that even if you look like a failure, you'd rejoice when they are strong in the Lord? Where do you need to repent, believe and fight to have a heart like Paul's for those you spiritually parent or encourage?

## TEST YOURSELF: *THE ULTIMATE REALITY CHECK*
## II Corinthians 13:1-10

*Reality Check #2: How do you know you're a Christian?*

By belief/faith    John 3:16, 20:31, Rom. 10:9-13, Eph. 2:8-9, I John 5:11-13

By Holy Spirit    Rom. 8:9, 15-16; I John 4:13

By love    I John 3:14, 4:7

By obedience    Matt. 7:21, I John 2:3-6, 3:6, 5:1-5

By fruit    Gal. 5:22-23, John 15:16

By suffering    Rom. 5:3-8, Phil. 3:8-10, 2 Tim. 1:8-12, I Pet. 4:12-14

## TRUST THE TRIUNE GOD
## II Corinthians 13:11-14

Why is the order of the final benediction important?

Do you daily experience the grace, love, peace, and fellowship of our Triune God?

## REALITY CHECK

Where is your heart? What do you want from people? What do you want for them? Are you willing to spend and be spent for those you have been called to spiritually encourage? How are you building others up and not tearing them down?

## REAL REALITY: SCRIPTURE MEDITATION

*BELIEVE IT. IT'S TRUE, AND TRUE FOR YOU. AMEN!*

*May the grace of the Lord Jesus Christ, and the love of God, and the fellowship of the Holy Spirit be with you all. II Corinthians 13:14*

# Reality Christianity:
# Radiating Christ in Our Cracked Lives

## Week 12: II Corinthians 12:11-13:14

*The Reality of REALigion / The Reality of Christ in Us*

## "Father" Paul Ends Letter with Reality Checks
## II Corinthians 12:11-13:14

Paul finishes this letter (the fourth written, second recorded) to his difficult spiritual children in Corinth with love, concern, warning, and blessing. This is Paul at his most vulnerable. He exposes his frustration (12:11), emphasizes his true authority (12:12, 13:10), reveals his father's heart for their souls (12:14-15), focuses on his real desire to build them up as the beloved (12:19, 13:10), states his fears for them (12:20-21), warns them what Christ will do to the unrepentant (13:1-4), challenges them to make sure they are in the faith (13:5), expresses his heart prayer for their restoration (13:6-9), and exhorts them to remember the main things and who is with them (13:11-14).

Paul gives the Corinthians two reality checks as he shows them real ministry and real faith. By personal example, he gives them a reality check on what authentic Christian ministry is: Christ's power in our weakness. In contrast, the super-apostles are distracting the Corinthians away from Christ and to themselves. They are burdening them for their money and confusing them with a different gospel, one with a self-focus instead of self-sacrifice focused on dependence on Christ alone. The second reality check Paul gives them (and a healthy one for all of us to consider) is to make sure they are in the faith (13:5). Paul wants them to remember the power and simplicity of the gospel and the mystery of what it means to be in Christ. The ending benediction (13:14) reflects our redemptive road: The grace of the Lord Jesus Christ opens the way to the love of God our Father and the fellowship of the Holy Spirit. The Triune God is with us and in us. There is no better truth. There is no "happier" ending.

## Reality Check #1: Are You in a Glad "Soul-Spending" Ministry?
## II Corinthians 12:11-21

Paul longs for his children to relish Jesus Christ and radiate him to a hurting world. He loves them so much that in their accusations of him he still reveals his heart for them: I want you, not your possessions. I will most gladly spend and be (entirely) spent for your souls. How about you? Real ministry is filled with exhaustion, misunderstandings, dry times when it seems your spiritual (and real!) children are sucking you dry but not pouring out. Paul expressed his frustration but comes back to the heart of his ministry: I will give my life for you for Christ's sake."As he was the Corinthians' spiritual father, selfless, other-directed sacrifice drove Paul's labors. He wanted nothing but them—their souls—for Christ. This is the hallmark of all true ministry at every level. . .True ministry selflessly seeks the spiritual welfare of others, gladly spending and being spent. . . . .This is what is most needed if authentic ministry is to take place—joyously seeking the best of others and gladly spending self."[105] So if you think you're "failing" this first test, Paul makes you realize who you really are in Christ (13:5), and what Christ's grace and power will do in your weakness (12:9, 13:14).

Paul role models this Christ-relishing, Christ-radiating ministry. Consider his words in these closing chapters of II Corinthians: I seek not what is yours but you (12:14). I will most gladly spend and be spent for your souls (12:15). Everything I do is for your strengthening and building up. I will remind you that you are beloved by the Lord and me (12:19). I will keep loving you even when criticized and falsely accused (12:11, 20). I will fear for you and grieve over your sin (12:20-21). I will speak truth and not spare those who are unrepentant in sin (13:1-4). I will challenge you to see if you are in Christ (13:5). I'm glad when I am weak or seem to fail if you're strong and pass the test (13:9). My prayer is for your restoration. I will come in the authority the Lord gave me for building you up, not tearing you down (13:10). I will bless you with the reality of the Triune God (13:14).

Paul is willing to fully expend himself in ministry because he knows whose he is, who he is following and knows he is in a battle for hearts and minds. Theodore Roosevelt knew that level of commitment when he stated, "It is not the critic who counts; not the man who points out how the strong man stumbles, or where the doer of deeds could have done them better. The credit belongs to the man who is actually in the arena, whose face is marred by dust and sweat and blood, who strives valiantly; who errs and comes short again and again; because there is not effort without error and shortcomings; but who does actually strive to do the deed; who knows the great enthusiasm, the great devotion, who spends himself in a worthy cause, who at the best knows in the end the triumph of high achievement and who at the worst, if he fails, at least he fails while daring greatly. So that his place shall never be with those cold and timid souls who know neither victory nor defeat."

This kind of authentic ministry is as John Piper states "to live gladly to make others glad in God."[106] He rails against the suburban ministry mindset of just helping others avoid sin and safely and comfortably get to the 'other side.' "How many lives are wasted by people who believe that the Christian life means simply avoiding badness and providing for the family. So, there is no adultery, no stealing, no killing, no embezzlement, no fraud—just lots of hard work during the day, and lots of TV and PG-13 videos in the evening (during quality family time), and lots of fun stuff on the weekend—woven around church

---

105 [1]R. Kent Hughes, *2 Corinthians: Power in Weakness* (Crossway Books: Wheaton, IL, 2006), 220.

106 John Piper, *Don't Waste Your Life* Crossway Books: Wheaton, IL, 2003), 102.

(mostly). This is life for millions of people. Wasted life. We were created for more, far more."[107] Paul's loving concern for the Corinthians was for them to refocus on reality, not be distracted by the promises of the super apostles or to live wasted, unrepentant lives. He reminds them who they really are. He wants to build them up, not tear them down. He wants to refocus them on the reality of their salvation through the Triune God by the grace of the Lord Jesus Christ (13:14).

## Reality Check #2: Are You "In" Christ?
## II Corinthians 13:1-10

How do you know you are in Christ?

It's as simple as your "ABCs."

A: *Acknowledge* that you are a sinner and helpless to save yourself (Rom. 3:23, 6:23). Jesus calls us to repent, to turn to him, which is accomplished only through his grace (Eph. 2:8-9) as a gift.

B: *Believe* in Jesus Christ alone for your salvation. John 20:31 summarizes John's gospel: *But these are written so that you may believe that Jesus is the Christ, the Son of God, and that by believing you may have life in his name.*

C: *Commit*. Surrender your life to God. Rest your full weight on him. Rom. 10:9-13 states, *If you confess with your mouth that Jesus is Lord and believe in your heart that God raised him from the dead, you will be saved. For with the heart one believes and is justified, and with the mouth one confesses and is saved. For the Scripture says, "Everyone who believes in him will not be put to shame." For there is no distinction between Jew and Greek; for the same Lord is Lord of all, bestowing his riches on all who call on him. For "everyone who calls on the name of the Lord will be saved."*

Return to the simple power of the gospel for salvation for everyone who believes (Rom. 1:16). That's what it means to be in Christ. But the depth of that new reconciled relationship will take us an eternity to grasp. Piper takes a stab at how big this gladness in our Triune God really is. It is a "gladness that has roots in God's eternal decree, was purchased by the blood of Christ, springs up in the newborn heart because of God's Spirit, awakens in repentance and faith, constitutes the essence of sanctification and Christlikeness, and gives rise to a life of love and a passion for redeeming the world after the image of God. Gladness in God is a *massive reality* planned and purchased and produced by God in the lives of his elect for the glory of his name."[108] Is your religion that REAL to you?

---

107 Piper, 119.

108 Piper, 104.

## Reality Check #3: Are You "In" the Reality of the Trinity?
## II Corinthians 13:11-14

Paul closes this letter with exhortations for all his brothers and sisters in Corinth and a benediction which magnifies the Triune God and the way of salvation.

Final words are always important. Consider the five imperatives Paul gives to the church: **Rejoice** as he anticipates repentance and restoration and reunion with his children. **Aim for restoration**. Paul's heart throughout this letter and especially in these last verses (12:19, 13:10-11) was for their upbuilding and restoration. In the Greek, this restoration has the image of putting back into place or mending, like fishing nets, an ongoing 'maintenance' work he calls them to do.

He then exhorts them to **comfort one another**, ending where he had begun (1:3-7) as we consider the God of love and peace and comfort. This image of "coming alongside" fits with his next call to **agree with one another**, something the Corinthians were not doing well. He was calling them to "unity in the apostolic truth that Paul had been teaching...they were to agree with one another on the main things, not everything. This meant that God's Word must be the standard and source of unity."[109] This is followed by the call to **live in peace**, wholeness, and acceptance of one another. These five form an "aggregate of five terse, staccato injunctions about rejoicing, restoring, comforting, agreeing, and living in peace—all present imperatives calling the Corinthians to continuous action day in and day out... In truth, therefore, the Christian life and the existence of unity within the church do not come through passivity. We must work at every aspect all the time. Restoration is work, comfort is work, agreement is work, peace is work, and even rejoicing requires thought and effort."[110]

Note the order of the benediction (13:14). It follows our Christian experience which starts with the grace of our Lord Jesus Christ, which opens us to the love of God and the fellowship of the Holy Spirit. "Grace is the means by which God's love reaches the believer (Rom. 8:39) ...and it is through the grace of Christ exhibited in the cross that God demonstrates his love (Rom. 5:8) and that believers came to participate in the Spirit's life and so form the community of the new Age."[111] It can also speak of the chronological order ... of the believer's experience of God: we come to Christ and so encounter God and then receive his Spirit."[112]

May you live in the reality of Paul's blessing: that the Triune God is with you to empower you in your weakness to live for him and glorify him. May you live in Christ, who though he was rich became poor for our sakes so that you too can gladly spend and be spent for peoples' souls.

---

109 Hughes, 233.

110 Hughes, 233.

111 [7] Murray J. Harris, *The Second Epistle to the Corinthians* (Eerdmans Publishing Co: Grand Rapids, MI, 2005), 938..

112 Harris, 938.

# Week 13: Reality Check
## Review of II Corinthians

**Review II Corinthians.** Look back to the outline of the study on pages 9–10, which lists each of the weekly studies and aims. Which lesson most impacted you and why?

II Corinthians reveals the real God in the middle of our "real" places. What attributes of God have stood out to you during this study? Why?

Did God reveal anything that surprised you or was new to you about himself through this study?

 Where do you need to trust who God is and rest in Him more? Which Scriptures about God and his promises to you do you need to believe in your life right now?

 List one or two attributes of God that you will seek to learn more about, meditate upon, and rest in more in the coming months.

**Look over II Corinthians** and the overview of the study. Paul shows us both the hard and holy realities of the Christian life in II Corinthians. As you review the hard realities Paul faced (the physical, mental, and spiritual sufferings; the attacks from the false apostles; the lack of appreciation and doubts about his credibility from the Corinthians; the longing and frustrations over the purity and unity of the Corinthian church; the spiritual battle with Satan; his own weaknesses and failings) which surprised you the most?

Which could you most identify with?

Which do you most fear experiencing?

Which hard realities are in your life right now?

How are you dealing with them?

How has God revealed himself to you or given you comfort, strength or truth in the midst of your hard realities?

 List your hardest reality and ask God to reveal Himself and give you hope and courage in the midst of it. Ask your group to pray for you.

**Review II Corinthians.** This book reveals that in the midst of some of our hardest realities we find the holiest realities (God's comfort in our suffering, God's faithfulness in our failure, God's ability in our inability, God's radiating through our brokenness, God's redemption of our pain, God's reconciliation of our lives and relationships, God's power in our weakness).

How have you been better able to grasp some of the "paradoxes" of the Christian life through this study and these Scriptures?

How has God revealed his holy realities in the midst of your hard realities?

 Write below how God has revealed more of what it is like to be a "real Christian" through this study of II Corinthians.

**Look over II Corinthians.** Paul reveals what it is like to truly love and minister to people, often very difficult people, as he reaches out to the Corinthians. What have you learned from Paul about what it means to truly love and minister to others in a reconciling, redemptive way?

 Where do you need God's strength and power in your weakness in ministry?

As you look at Paul's life and example, where do you most need God to show up in your life as you relate to others?

 Who is God calling you to minister to? Are you willing to spend and expend yourself? Pray that God will show you who to minister to and how to rely on Him in your ministry.

**Read II Corinthians 13:1-11.** Paul ends his letter to the Corinthians challenging them to examine themselves to make sure they are in the faith.

As we finish this study, test yourself: Are you in Christ? How do you know?

Pray through the following Scriptures as you examine the evidence of the Christian life:

**Faith:** John 3:16, 20:31; Romans 10:9-13; Ephesians 2:8-9

**Holy Spirit:** Romans 8:9, 15-16; I John 4:13

**Love:** I John 3:14, 4:7

**Obedience:** Matthew 7:21, I John 2:3-6, 3:6, 5:1-5, 18

**Fruit:** Galatians 5:22-23, John 15:16

If Christ is in you, His resurrected power indwells you. As you finish this study, where do you want Him to most transform you?

 Where do you need to change your priorities so you can relish and radiate the real Christ more? What needs to change to make your Christianity more real to yourself and those around you?

## *Week 13: Review*
## II Corinthians

**REALITY CHECKS**

**THE GOALS OF THE STUDY**

✓ RELISH THE REAL JESUS CHRIST

*How have you seen or "relished" Jesus Christ more through the study of II Corinthians?*

✓ RADIATE CHRIST THROUGH YOUR CRACKED LIVES

*Where have you let down some of your "veils" or shown some of your cracks to let Christ radiate through you to others through this study?*

✓ REJOICE IN THE REAL MINISTRY OF GOD'S POWER IN YOUR WEAKNESS
*How have you begun to grasp the reality of Christian ministry and experienced God's power in your weakness?*

# Reality Christianity:
# Radiating Christ in Our Cracked Lives

## Week 13: Reality Check

*Are You Living in Reality?*

## Reality Christianity: Relishing and Radiating Christ in Our Cracked Lives

The goals of this 13-week study of II Corinthians is that you will more and more see and relish the real Jesus Christ and radiate Him through the cracks in your lives and rejoice in the real ministry of God's power in your weakness. In your personal study of Paul's most personal and vulnerable of letters, in the times of teaching, and in your small groups, has God given you hope and hunger for more of his holy Word, for more of his Holy Spirit and more of his holy people? Have you gotten a whiff of the fragrance of Christ? Have you seen his radiance through your own cracks and through others' lives? Have you tasted the reality of a ministry of being gladly spent for Christ and for others, even when under criticism or comparison? That's my heart for you.

When you grasp that it really is all about Christ in you and his power resting on you in your ongoing weakness, you're beginning to live the mystery and freedom of the gospel. When you realize you give more hope to those around you, not by holding it all together and serving out of your competencies, but by allowing Christ to radiate through your cracked lives and unveiled weaknesses, you're beginning to live in reality. Jesus Christ is Reality.

## Reality Check #1: The Reality of God

Paul balances his personal reality with the reality of who God is. When you are plunging in deep and hard realities, your anchor is the character of God. When you feel confused about his promises, when the Lie Guy laughs in your ear, when you feel fearful or abandoned, believe the truth of his Word and his character. Through these chapters, Paul is revealing God as the Father of compassion and the God of all comfort (1:3); our faithful God (1:18;) Jesus as the Yes and Amen (1:20); the Spirit as our Guarantee and Seal and Life-giver (122, 3:6); Jesus as our confidence and competence (3:4-6); our Lord who is Spirit, freedom and glorious (3:17-18); our all-surpassing powerful and radiant God who is light and glory (4:6-7); eternal and unseen (4:18); the resurrected, living, loving Christ (5:14-15); the righteous, reconciling One made to be sin for us (5:21); our relational and redeeming God committed to his people (6:16); our saving, sorrowing God (7:10); our enriching, rich-yet-becoming-poor-for-us God (8:9); our aboundingly able, grace-giving God (9:8); the Indescribable Gift (9:15); authoritative and building-up God (10:4, 8); our true God and true husband Jesus Christ (11:2); the grace and power of Jesus, the

Sufficient One (12:9); crucified and resurrected, alive, and powerful, Christ in you (13:4-5); and the grace, love, and fellowship of the Triune God (13:14).

Believe these unchanging truths of God in the midst of your hard realities. Live in Reality.

## Reality Check #2: Hard Realities/Holy Realities

Paul faced realities beyond what most of us can conceive of enduring from without and within. Think through Paul's physical, mental, and spiritual sufferings; the attacks from the false apostles; the lack of appreciation and doubts about his credibility from his own spiritual children in Corinth; the longings and frustrations over the purity and unity of the Corinthian church and needs of the saints in Jerusalem; the spiritual battle with Satan; his own weakness; the gracious "no" he received from God as he begged for release from his thorn; his endurance in loving those who did not love in return; and being caught between longing for heaven and ministering for those who were God's own in this world. Now, realizing that all that Paul desired was to point to Christ, read through that list again and substitute Jesus Christ's name. Meditate on the hard realities Jesus Christ endured as he became sin for us, separated from his Father, enduring the cross in weakness, all for our sake. Consider Jesus Christ, resurrected in power and living in us, interceding for us, coming alongside us in our suffering, leading us in triumph. Our comfort in our hard realities is that Jesus went before us, endured beyond what we can conceive, and became poor so we could become rich, so that our ultimate treasure is Christ radiating in and through our cracked pots. Jesus identifies with us, yet without sin and failure. Therefore, his sacrifice is sufficient. Thanks be to God for his indescribable gift. II Corinthians shows us Jesus Christ, our Sufficiency. Live in Reality.

## Reality Check #3: Real Ministry

Reading II Corinthians makes you recognize the paradox of Christian life and ministry: that it is through our weakness that God reveals his power and grace, in our suffering we experience the God who comforts, in our failure and inability, we experience God's faithfulness and ability, in our brokenness, Christ's light radiates. We enter in with Christ as his ambassadors in his reconciling and redeeming ministry as broken people to a broken world. That is how we give hope. That is how we point to the Reality of Jesus Christ.

The message of II Corinthians is summed up in Jesus' words in II Cor. 12:9: *My grace is sufficient for you, for my power is made perfect in weakness.* Are you willing to minister from weakness to gladly spend and be spent for others souls? Answer his call. Live in Reality.

## Reality Check #4: Christ in You

Paul concludes with Ultimate Reality when he challenges and reminds the Corinthians to test themselves to see if they are in the faith (13:5) and in Jesus Christ. Are you in Jesus Christ? Is your religion REAL?

Take a moment now to take the simple test of faith, which is as simple as your "ABCs."

**A:** *Acknowledge* that you are a sinner and helpless to save yourself (Rom 3:23, 6:23). Jesus calls us to repent, to turn to him, which is accomplished only through his grace (Eph 2:8-9) as a gift.

**B:** *Believe* in Jesus Christ alone for your salvation. John 20:31 summarizes John's gospel: *But these are written so that you may believe that Jesus is the Christ, the Son of God, and that by believing you may have life in his name.*

**C:** *Commit.* Surrender your life to Jesus Christ. Rest your full weight on him. Say Yes to the Bridegroom, to the One who died for you, the One who is Yes to all God's promises. Rom. 10:9-13 states, *If you confess with your mouth that Jesus is Lord and believe in your heart that God raised him from the dead, you will be saved. For with the heart one believes and is justified, and with the mouth one confesses and is saved. For the Scripture says, "Everyone who believes in him will not be put to shame." For there is no distinction between Jew and Greek; for the same Lord is Lord of all, bestowing his riches on all who call on him. For "everyone who calls on the name of the Lord will be saved* That's what it means to be in Christ. You are then God's reconciled child (II Cor. 5:21) and his love compels you (5:14). This life is lived out in a fallen world where you will continue to struggle with weakness and Christ's power will continue to rest on you. As a Christian, your true identity is as God's beloved (7:1) as the temple of the living God (6:16) and the Lord Almighty will be a father to you, and you shall be his sons and daughters (6:18). Relish Paul's last benediction (13:14) as you go forward in real ministry and Live in Reality!

> **May the grace of the Lord Jesus Christ,**
> *and the love of God,*
> *and the fellowship of the Holy Spirit*
> *be with you all.*

*ESV Study Bible* (Crossways Bibles: Wheaton, IL, 2008), 2220.

# With Gratitude

Often, I've thought something's wrong with me. Why was being a Christian so much harder for me? "Other folks" seemed to have it all together. Their Plan A's fell into place. They knew the answers. They didn't seem to mess up like me in relationships or ministry.

In the ugliness of my whining and comparing, God graciously led me to II Corinthians. There's no book like it which reveals the reality of what it means to be a Christian, live in relationship with other Christians, and to minister out of weakness, not strength.

Thank you, Paul, for this most raw and real letter. Thanks to all you who have dropped your veils and revealed what it's like to be a "real" Christian. Thanks to Bible Study Fellowship for showing me the power of Scripture to transform lives and teaching me to dig deep. God blessed me through many professors at Beeson Divinity School, especially Dr. Robert Smith, Jr., who helped me believe that our Messiah came for messes like me. Thanks to Dr. Bob Flayhart for teaching me the three-step waltz of repent, believe, and fight. Thanks to Chris and Mary Granberry of Sacred Road Ministries on the Yakama Indian Reservation who live out the real and hard of ministry with God's grace. Thanks to my own "Get Real" circle of dear friends.

Most of all thanks to my children, Winn and Christa, and especially to Bill, for loving me in all of my realities.

My prayer is that we all will be compelled by the love of Christ.

Nancy

# Personal and Group Prayer Journal

*Please use the following blank sheets to record and follow up on prayer requests for you and your group members and personal "takeaways" from the weekly lessons.*

# Personal and Group Prayer Journal

*Please use the following blank sheets to record and follow up on prayer requests for you and your group members and personal "takeaways" from the weekly lessons.*

## Personal and Group Prayer Journal

*Please use the following blank sheets to record and follow up on prayer requests for you and your group members and personal "takeaways" from the weekly lessons.*

## Personal and Group Prayer Journal

*Please use the following blank sheets to record and follow up on prayer requests for you and your group members and personal "takeaways" from the weekly lessons.*

# Personal and Group Prayer Journal

*Please use the following blank sheets to record and follow up on prayer requests for you and your group members and personal "takeaways" from the weekly lessons.*

# Personal and Group Prayer Journal

*Please use the following blank sheets to record and follow up on prayer requests for you and your group members and personal "takeaways" from the weekly lessons.*

## Personal and Group Prayer Journal

*Please use the following blank sheets to record and follow up on prayer requests for you and your group members and personal "takeaways" from the weekly lessons.*

Made in the USA
Columbia, SC
13 September 2022

67169135R00152